Collins

TREASURE HOUSE

Teacher's Guide 5
Comprehension Skills

Author: Abigail Steel

William Collins' dream of knowledge for all began with the publication of his first book in 1819.

A self-educated mill worker, he not only enriched millions of lives, but also founded a flourishing publishing house. Today, staying true to this spirit, Collins books are packed with inspiration, innovation and practical expertise. They place you at the centre of a world of possibility and give you exactly what you need to explore it.

Collins. Freedom to teach.

Published by Collins
An imprint of HarperCollins*Publishers*
The News Building
1 London Bridge Street
London
SE1 9GF

Browse the complete Collins catalogue at
www.collins.co.uk

© HarperCollins*Publishers* Limited 2017

10 9 8 7 6 5 4 3 2 1

ISBN 978-0-00-822294-9

All rights reserved. No part of this publication may be reproduced, stored in a retrieval system, or transmitted in any form by any means, electronic, mechanical, photocopying, recording or otherwise, without the prior written permission of the Publisher or a licence permitting restricted copying in the United Kingdom issues by the Copyright Licensing Agency Ltd., 90 Tottenham Court Road, London W1T 4LP.

British Library Cataloguing in Publication Data

A catalogue record for this publication is available from the British Library.

Publishing Director: Lee Newman
Publishing Manager: Helen Doran
Senior Editor: Hannah Dove
Project Manager: Emily Hooton
Author: Abigail Steel
Development Editor: Hannah Hirst-Dunton
Copy-editor: Ros and Chris Davies
Proofreader: Tracy Thomas
Cover design and artwork: Amparo Barrera and Ken Vail Graphic Design
Internal design concept: Amparo Barrera
Typesetter: Jouve India Private Ltd
Illustrations: Alberto Saichann (Beehive Illustration)
Production Controller: Rachel Weaver

Printed and bound by
CPI Group (UK) Ltd, Croydon, CR0 4YY

Acknowledgements

The publishers wish to thank the following for permission to reproduce content. Every effort has been made to trace copyright holders and to obtain their permission for the use of copyright materials. The publishers will gladly receive any information enabling them to rectify any error or omission at the first opportunity.

David Higham Associates Ltd for extracts on pages 25-27 from *The Chicken Gave it to Me* by Anne Fine, Egmont, 2007. Reproduced by permission of David Higham Associates Ltd; Lord Alfred Douglas Literary Estate for the poem on pages 34-36 "The Shark" by Lord Alfred Douglas, copyright © Literary Executors of the Estate of Lord Alfred Douglas. All rights reserved; David Higham Associates Limited for the poem on pages 37-39 "Colonel Fazackerley" by Charles Causley, from *Collected Poems for Children*, Macmillan Children's Books, 2008. Reproduced by permission of David Higham Associates Ltd; Aitken Alexander Associates Ltd for extracts on pages 44-46 and 100 from *The Borrowers* by Mary Norton, first published by J.M. Dent and Sons Ltd, copyright © Mary Norton. Reproduced with permission from Aitken Alexander Associates Ltd; and HarperCollins Publishers Ltd for extracts on pages 47-49 and 101 from *The Lost Gardens* by Philip Osment, copyright © 2011, Philip Osment. Reproduced by permission of HarperCollins Publishers Ltd.

Contents

About Treasure House 4

Support, embed and challenge 12

Assessment 13

Support with teaching comprehension 14

Delivering the 2014 National Curriculum for English 16

Unit 1: Fiction: 'A Clever Way to Catch a Thief' 22

Unit 2: Fiction: 'I Go Chicken-Dippy' 25

Unit 3: Fiction (classic): 'Robinson Crusoe' 28

Unit 4: Non-fiction (news report): 'Cubs and Brownies to the rescue' 31

Unit 5: Poetry: 'The Shark' 34

Unit 6: Poetry: 'Colonel Fazackerley' 37

Unit 7: Non-fiction (formal letter): 'Noisy neighbour' 40

Review unit 1: Fiction (classic): 'Pinocchio' 43

Unit 8: Fiction (classic): 'The Borrowers' 44

Unit 9: Playscript: 'The Lost Gardens' 47

Unit 10: Poetry: 'A Smuggler's Song' 50

Unit 11: Poetry: 'From a Railway Carriage' 53

Unit 12: Non-fiction (instructions): 'Magic matchsticks' 56

Unit 13: Non-fiction (historical): 'The Trojan War' 59

Unit 14: Fiction (legend): 'Shen Nung' 62

Review unit 2: Non-fiction (information text): 'Your Brain' 65

Unit 15: Non-fiction (biography): 'Barack Obama' 66

Unit 16: Fiction (modern): 'The Hedgehog Mystery' 69

Unit 17: Fiction (traditional tale): 'The Dragon Pearl' 72

Unit 18: Poetry: 'What on Earth?' and 'Progress Man!' 75

Unit 19: Non-fiction (information text): 'How to be an Ancient Greek in 25 easy stages' 78

Unit 20: Non-fiction (autobiography): 'Ade Adepitan: A Paralympian's Story' 81

Review unit 3: Poetry: 'Summer Afternoon' and 'Gathering in the Days' 84

Photocopiable resources 85

About Treasure House

Treasure House is a comprehensive and flexible bank of books and online resources for teaching the English curriculum. The Treasure House series offers two different pathways: one covering each English strand discretely (Skills Focus Pathway) and one integrating texts and the strands to create a programme of study (Integrated English Pathway). This Teacher's Guide is part of the Skills Focus Pathway.

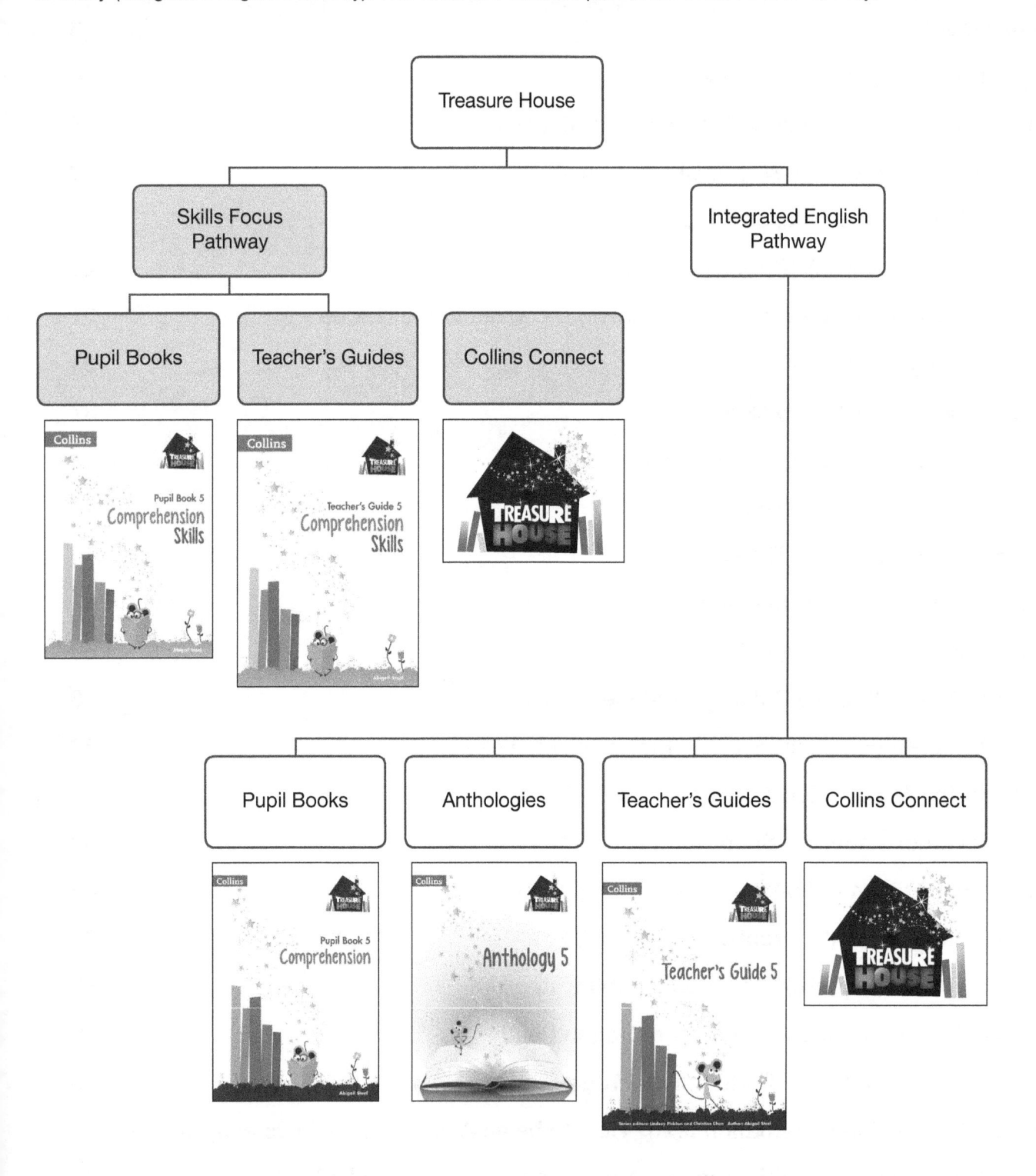

About Treasure House

1. Skills Focus

The Skills Focus Pupil Books and Teacher's Guides for all four strands (Comprehension; Spelling; Composition; and Vocabulary, Grammar and Punctuation) allow you to teach each curriculum area in a targeted way. Each unit in the Pupil Book is mapped directly to the statutory requirements of the National Curriculum. Each Teacher's Guide provides step-by-step instructions to guide you through the Pupil Book activities and digital Collins Connect resources for each competency. With a clear focus on skills and clearly-listed curriculum objectives you can select the appropriate resources to support your lessons.

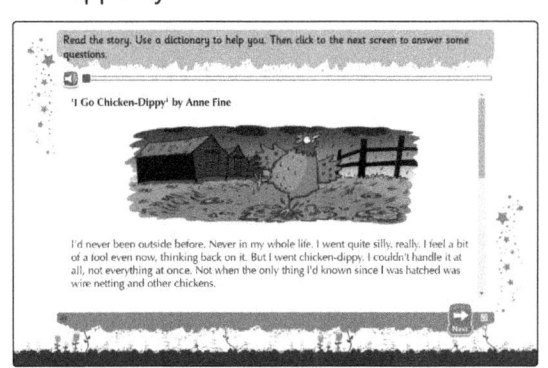

2. Integrated English

Alternatively, the Integrated English pathway offers a complete programme of genre-based teaching sequences. There is one Teacher's Guide and one Anthology for each year group. Each Teacher's Guide provides 15 teaching sequences focused on different genres of text such as fairy tales, letters and newspaper articles. The Anthologies contain the classic texts, fiction, non-fiction and poetry required for each sequence. Each sequence also weaves together all four dimensions of the National Curriculum for English – Comprehension; Spelling; Composition; and Vocabulary, Grammar and Punctuation – into a complete English programme. The Pupil Books and Collins Connect provide targeted explanation of key points and practice activities organised by strand. This programme provides 30 weeks of teaching inspiration.

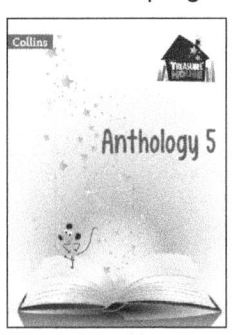

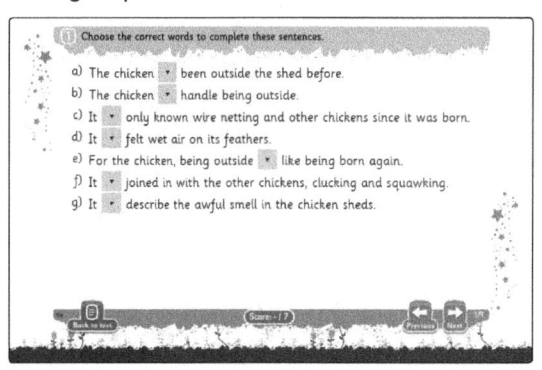

Other components

Handwriting Books, Handwriting Workbooks, Word Books and the online digital resources on Collins Connect are suitable for use with both pathways.

About Treasure House

Treasure House Skills Focus Teacher's Guides

Year	Comprehension	Composition	Vocabulary, Grammar and Punctuation	Spelling
1	978-0-00-822290-1	978-0-00-822302-1	978-0-00-822296-3	978-0-00-822308-3
2	978-0-00-822291-8	978-0-00-822303-8	978-0-00-822297-0	978-0-00-822309-0
3	978-0-00-822292-5	978-0-00-822304-5	978-0-00-822298-7	978-0-00-822310-6
4	978-0-00-822293-2	978-0-00-822305-2	978-0-00-822299-4	978-0-00-822311-3
5	978-0-00-822294-9	978-0-00-822306-9	978-0-00-822300-7	978-0-00-822312-0
6	978-0-00-822295-6	978-0-00-822307-6	978-0-00-822301-4	978-0-00-822313-7

About Treasure House

Inside the Skills Focus Teacher's Guides

The teaching notes in each unit in the Teacher's Guide provide you with subject information or background, a range of whole class and differentiated activities including photocopiable resource sheets and links to the Pupil Book and the online Collins Connect activities.

Each **Overview** provides clear objectives for each lesson tied into the new curriculum, links to the other relevant components and a list of any additional resources required.

Teaching overview provides a brief introduction to the specific skill concept or text type and some pointers on how to approach it.

Support, embed & challenge supports a mastery approach with activities provided at three levels.

Introduce the concept/text provides 5–10 minutes of preliminary discussion points or class/group activities to get the pupils engaged in the lesson focus and set out any essential prior learning.

Pupil practice gives guidance and the answers to each of the three sections in the Pupil Book: *Get started*, *Try these* and *Now try these*.

Homework / Additional activities lists ideas for classroom or homework activities, and relevant activities from Collins Connect.

Two photocopiable **resource** worksheets per unit provide extra practice of the specific lesson concept. They are designed to be used with the activities in support, embed or challenge sections.

About Treasure House

Treasure House Skills Focus Pupil Books

There are four Skills Focus Pupil Books for each year group, based on the four dimensions of the National Curriculum for English: Comprehension; Spelling; Composition; and Vocabulary, Grammar and Punctuation. The Pupil Books provide a child-friendly introduction to each subject and a range of initial activities for independent pupil-led learning. A Review unit for each term assesses pupils' progress.

Year	Comprehension	Composition	Vocabulary, Grammar and Punctuation	Spelling
1	978-0-00-823634-2	978-0-00-823646-5	978-0-00-823640-3	978-0-00-823652-6
2	978-0-00-823635-9	978-0-00-823647-2	978-0-00-823641-0	978-0-00-823653-3
3	978-0-00-823636-6	978-0-00-823648-9	978-0-00-823642-7	978-0-00-823654-0
4	978-0-00-823637-3	978-0-00-823649-6	978-0-00-823643-4	978-0-00-823655-7
5	978-0-00-823638-0	978-0-00-823650-2	978-0-00-823644-1	978-0-00-823656-4
6	978-0-00-823639-7	978-0-00-823651-9	978-0-00-823645-8	978-0-00-823657-1

About Treasure House

Inside the Skills Focus Pupil Books

Comprehension

Includes high-quality text extracts covering poetry, prose, traditional tales, playscripts and non-fiction.

Pupils retrieve and record information, learn to draw inferences from texts and increase their familiarity with a wide range of literary genres.

Composition

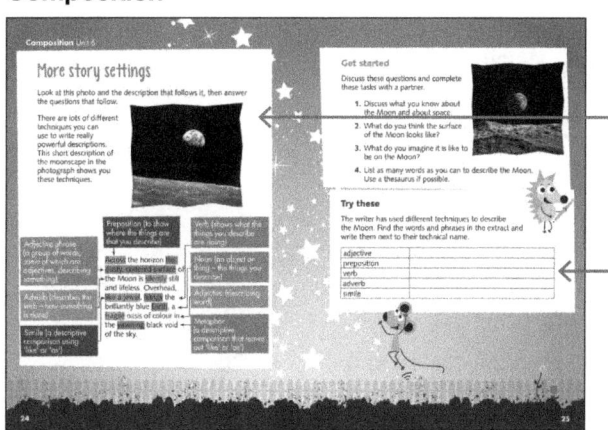

Includes high-quality, annotated text extracts as models for different types of writing.

Children learn how to write effectively and for a purpose.

Vocabulary, Grammar and Punctuation

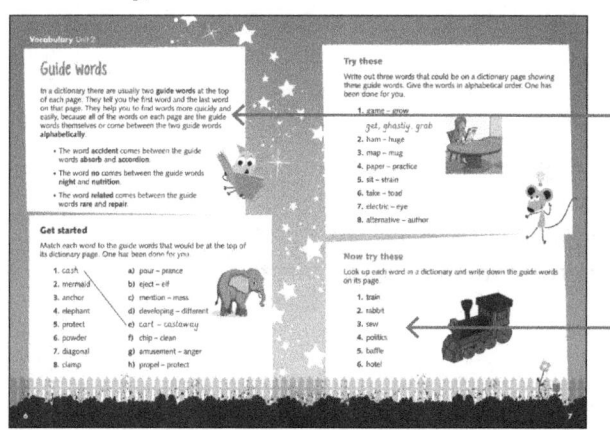

Develops children's knowledge and understanding of grammar and punctuation skills.

A rule is introduced and explained. Children are given lots of opportunities to practise using it.

Spelling

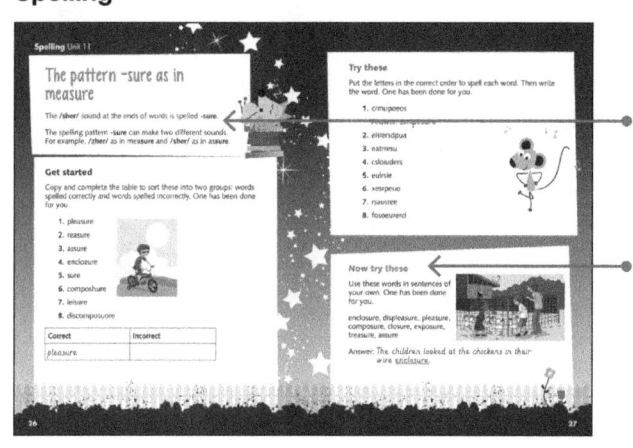

Spelling rules are introduced and explained.

Practice is provided for spotting and using the spelling rules, correcting misspelt words and using the words in context.

About Treasure House

Treasure House on Collins Connect

Digital resources for Treasure House are available on Collins Connect which provides a wealth of interactive activities. Treasure House is organised into six core areas on Collins Connect:

- Comprehension
- Spelling
- Composition
- Vocabulary, Grammar and Punctuation
- The Reading Attic
- Teacher's Guides and Anthologies.

For most units in the Skills Focus Pupil Books, there is an accompanying Collins Connect unit focused on the same teaching objective. These fun, independent activities can be used for initial pupil-led learning, or for further practice using a different learning environment. Either way, with Collins Connect, you have a wealth of questions to help children embed their learning.

Treasure House on Collins Connect is available via subscription at connect.collins.co.uk

Features of Treasure House on Collins Connect

The digital resources enhance children's comprehension, spelling, composition, and vocabulary, grammar, punctuation skills through providing:

- a bank of varied and engaging interactive activities so children can practise their skills independently
- audio support to help children access the texts and activities
- auto-mark functionality so children receive instant feedback and have the opportunity to repeat tasks.

Teachers benefit from useful resources and time-saving tools including:

- teacher-facing materials such as audio and explanations for front-of-class teaching or pupil-led learning
- lesson starter videos for some Composition units
- downloadable teaching notes for all online activities
- downloadable teaching notes for Skills Focus and Integrated English pathways
- the option to assign homework activities to your classes
- class records to monitor progress.

Comprehension

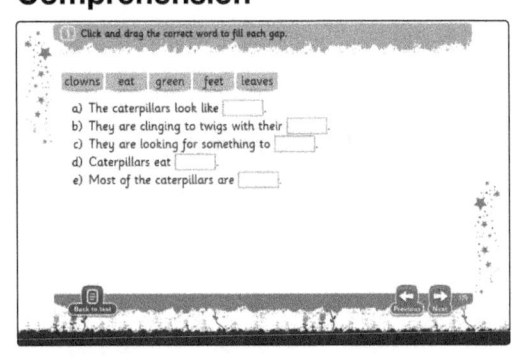

- Includes high-quality text extracts covering poetry, prose, traditional tales, playscripts and non-fiction.
- Audio function supports children to access the text and the activities

Composition

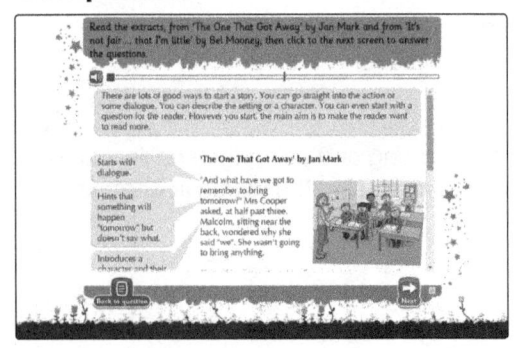

- Activities support children to develop and build more sophisticated sentence structures.
- Every unit ends with a longer piece of writing that can be submitted to the teacher for marking.

About Treasure House

Vocabulary, Grammar and Punctuation

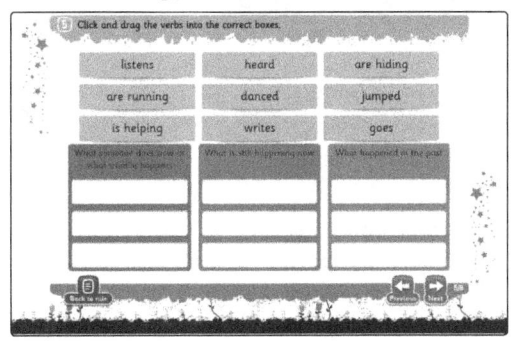

- Fun, practical activities develop children's knowledge and understanding of grammar and punctuation skills.
- Each skill is reinforced with a huge, varied bank of practice questions.

Spelling

- Fun, practical activities develop children's knowledge and understanding of each spelling rule.
- Each rule is reinforced with a huge, varied bank of practice questions.
- Children spell words using an audio prompt, write their own sentences and practise spelling using Look Say Cover Write Check.

Reading Attic

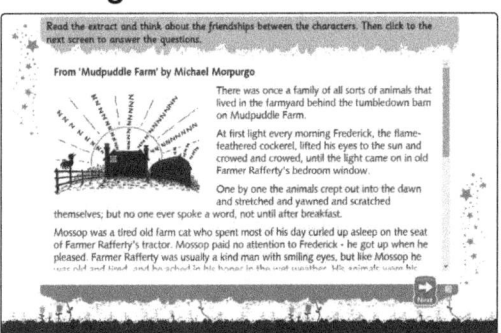

- Children's love of reading is nurtured with texts from exciting children's authors including Micheal Bond, David Walliams and Micheal Morpurgo.
- Lesson sequences accompany the texts, with drama opportunities and creative strategies for engaging children with key themes, characters and plots.
- Whole-book projects encourage reading for pleasure.

Treasure House Digital Teacher's Guides and Anthologies

The teaching sequences and anthology texts for each year group are included as a flexible bank of resources.

The teaching notes for each skill strand and year group are also included on Collins Connect.

Support, embed and challenge

Treasure House provides comprehensive, detailed differentiation at three levels to ensure that all children are able to access achievement. It is important that children master the basic skills before they go further in their learning. Children may make progress towards the standard at different speeds, with some not reaching it until the very end of the year.

In the Teacher's Guide, Support, Embed and Challenge sections allow teachers to keep the whole class focussed with no child left behind. Two photocopiable resources per unit offer additional material linked to the Support, Embed or Challenge sections.

Support

The Support section offers simpler or more scaffolded activities that will help learners who have not yet grasped specific concepts covered. Background information may also be provided to help children to contextualise learning. This enables children to make progress so that they can keep up with the class.

To help with reading comprehension, some support activities help learners to access the core text, for example, by giving some background information to the story or support with figurative speech. This is more motivating and enjoyable than offering a simplified text.

If you have a teaching assistant, you may wish to ask him or her to help children work through these activities. You might then ask children who have completed these activities to progress to other more challenging tasks found in the Embed or Challenge sections – or you may decide more practice of the basics is required. Collins Connect can provide further activities.

Embed

The Embed section includes activities to embed learning and is aimed at those who children who are working at the expected standard. It ensures that learners have understood key teaching objectives for the age-group. These activities could be used by the whole class or groups, and most are appropriate for both teacher-led and independent work.

In Comprehension, all children should cross the threshold of reading the texts in Treasure House; however, the depth of their analysis and understanding will vary depending on prior experience, current interests and motivation. Activities in the Embed section encourage children to apply their learning by further analysing the text or by planning their own writing based on the same theme or text-type.

Challenge

The Challenge section provides additional tasks, questions or activities that will push children who have mastered the concept without difficulty. This keeps children motivated and allows them to gain a greater depth of understanding. You may wish to give these activities to fast finishers to work through independently.

In Comprehension, children explore the text-type or theme further through drama, research, discussion or by doing their own writing.

Assessment

Teacher's Guides

There are opportunities for assessment throughout the Treasure House series. The teaching notes in Treasure House Teacher's Guides offer ideas for questions, informal assessment and spelling tests.

Pupil Book Review units

Each Pupil Book has three Review units designed as a quick formative assessment tool for the end of each term. Questions assess the work that has been covered over the previous units. These review units will provide you with an informal way of measuring your pupils' progress. You may wish to use these as Assessment for Learning to help you and your pupils to understand where they are in their learning journey.

The Review units in the Comprehension Pupil Books provide children with a new text or extract to read and understand. Children can draw on what they have learned during the term to help them access the new text without an initial teaching session to guide them. Questions types may reoccur across the Review units allowing you to see progression across the year, and the three reviews will always cover all three genres: fiction, non-fiction and poetry.

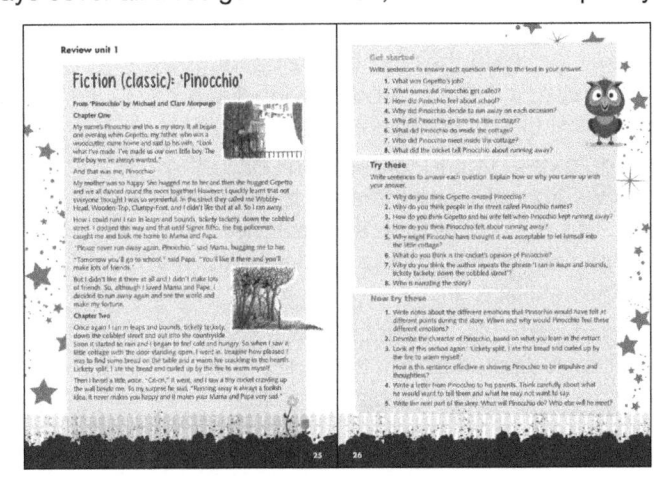

Assessment in Collins Connect

Activities on Collins Connect can also be used for effective assessment. Activities with auto-marking mean that if children answer incorrectly, they can make another attempt helping them to analyse their own work for mistakes. Homework activities can also be assigned to classes through Collins Connect. At the end of activities, children can select a smiley face to indicate how they found the task giving you useful feedback on any gaps in knowledge.

Class records on Collins Connect allow you to get an overview of children's progress with several features. You can choose to view records by unit, pupil or strand. By viewing detailed scores, you can view pupils' scores question by question in a clear table-format to help you establish areas where there might be particular strengths and weaknesses both class-wide and for individuals.

If you wish, you can also set mastery judgements (mastery achieved and exceeded, mastery achieved, mastery not yet achieved) to help see where your children need more help.

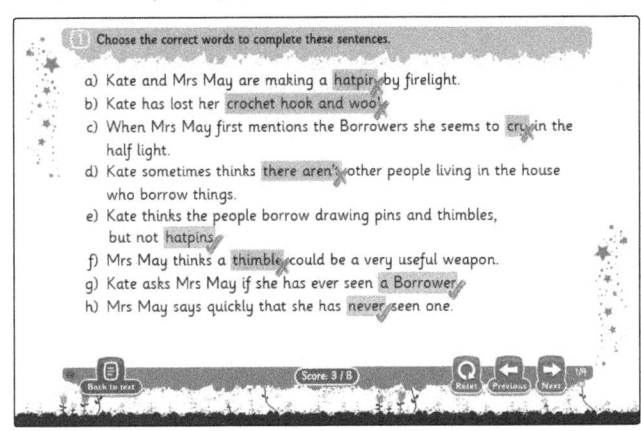

Support with teaching comprehension

The teacher's guides for Comprehension units can be followed in a simple linear fashion that structures the lesson into five sections:

- assessment of existing skills and knowledge, and an introduction to the unit's source text
- reading the source text
- completion of the 'pupil practice' questions
- differentiated work, following the Support, Embed and Challenge activity guidance (using the provided photocopiable worksheets)
- homework or additional activities.

However, this lesson structure is intended to be flexible. While we recommend that the first three of these steps should usually be followed in the given order, work following the pupil practice questions can be manipulated in numerous ways to suit the needs, skills and preferences of your class.

For example, you may wish to set one of the differentiation activities as homework for the whole class, or to guide children through an 'additional' activity during the lesson, rather than setting it as homework. You may alternatively judge that your class has firmly grasped the concept being taught, and choose not to use any activity suggested, or perhaps introduce only the Extend activity: it is not essential that every activity outlined in the teacher's guide units should be completed.

With the same motivation, many activities (and worksheets) could be adapted for reuse in units other than the one for which they are provided. Several activity and worksheet types are already repeated in similar forms between (and sometimes within) year groups. This is in order both to show the children's changing levels of attainment directly, and to allow any children who have found an activity challenging to reattempt it in a new context after developing their skills.

If, however, children find a particular activity either challenging or particularly engaging, you should also feel free to repeat that activity, where appropriate, at your own discretion. For example, if children enjoy considering appropriate costumes and settings when looking at a playscript (an activity, with worksheet, suggested in Year 3 Unit 17), this activity could be adapted to fit any playscript source text – and many prose fiction texts, too.

You may also wish to consider using Support activities in conjunction with the pupil practice questions, if children are struggling with content or a concept with which the Support activity deals. For example, if questions within the 'Try these' and 'Now try these' sections of pupil practice require understanding of similes, you may wish to intervene and prepare children using an appropriate Support activity (such as suggested in Year 3 Unit 2).

By using the teacher's guide units and their suggested activities flexibly, you can choose to tailor the resources at your fingertips to provide the most beneficial learning system for the children being taught.

Teaching comprehension is a key part of achieving the universal aim of developing children's love of literature through widespread reading for enjoyment. If children are confident and fluent readers, who understand the form and content of the texts they read they are more likely to enjoy them.

We can make learning comprehension easy and fun by employing simple techniques to guide children along their reading journey.

Modelling

When reading a letter or newspaper article to the class remember to hesitate on words that they might not know, intimate that you are unsure of the proper meaning and look them up in a dictionary. You might also model how you use context or grammar clues to work out the meaning using the rest of the text.

Making predictions

When embarking on any new text ask children to consider what they think it will be about, or what they think might happen. Show how to look for clues in the presentation of the text or the introductory information you have. Remember to model making your own predictions too – this gives you an opportunity to demonstrate how to rationalize a prediction by speaking your thought processes aloud.

Questioning

Questioning can take many forms and penetrate many depths of understanding. Questions can be closed, requiring short, defined answers or they can be open, enabling the children to explore wider thoughts. Sometimes the best questions are those that are spontaneous and form part of a natural conversation exploring a text. Encourage children to form their own questions about the purpose, structure and content of texts – they could note these down and return to them later to see if they have discovered the answers after reading.

Retelling and summarizing

Encourage children to reflect upon what has happened in a text – this can be a surprisingly challenging activity. Provide plenty of demonstrations of how to retell and summarize. Retelling and summarizing can take many fun, interactive forms such as role play, radio presentations, creating news flash articles, and oral story retellings. Some children struggle with sequencing and ordering so build this in with your retelling activities.

Visualizing

When we read we create mental images of what is happening. Descriptions of people, places and action are acted out in our minds. For children this skill doesn't always come naturally. Ask children to close their eyes and focus on imagining how something looks. Compare written texts to the films and TV shows they are familiar with watching. Point out specific adjectives and adverbs that are actively working within the text to assist the reader. Enable children the opportunity to draw and paint their interpretations of the texts they read.

Connections to children's own experiences

Younger children are often better at pointing at when they recognise a similarity between their own life and something they read in a text. Older children tend to become less inward looking and aren't so forthcoming with the links they make to texts. Encourage them by asking direct questions: *Does anyone else recognise this event? Do you know a character like this? Have you ever been to a similar place? When have you felt that emotion like the character?* Making explicit connections with the text can advance children's understanding of not only the event being described but also the history to the event and the character's emotions. They are able to talk about the 'bigger picture'.

Delivering the 2014 National Curriculum for English

English Programme of Study		Units																			
Reading – comprehension		1	2	3	4	5	6	7	8	9	10	11	12	13	14	15	16	17	18	19	20
Maintain positive attitudes to reading and understanding of what they read by:	Continuing to read and discuss an increasingly wide range of fiction, poetry, plays, non-fiction and reference books or textbooks	✓	✓	✓	✓	✓	✓	✓	✓	✓	✓	✓	✓	✓	✓	✓	✓	✓	✓	✓	✓
	Reading books that are structured in different ways and reading for a range of purposes				✓			✓					✓	✓		✓				✓	✓
	Increasing their familiarity with a wide range of books, including myths, legends and traditional stories, modern fiction, fiction from our literary heritage, and books from other cultures and traditions					✓				✓					✓			✓			
	Recommending books that they have read to their peers, giving reasons for their choices	✓		✓			✓		✓						✓		✓	✓			
	Identifying and discussing themes and conventions in and across a wide range of writing	✓	✓	✓	✓		✓	✓	✓	✓	✓	✓	✓	✓	✓	✓	✓	✓	✓	✓	✓
	Making comparisons within and across books	✓	✓												✓	✓	✓	✓			
	Learning a wider range of poetry by heart					✓	✓				✓	✓							✓		
	Preparing poems and plays to read aloud and to perform, showing understanding through intonation, tone and volume so that the meaning is clear to an audience					✓	✓			✓	✓	✓							✓		

English Programme of Study

Reading – comprehension

Understand what they read by:	1	2	3	4	5	6	7	8	9	10	11	12	13	14	15	16	17	18	19	20
Checking that the book makes sense to them, discussing their understanding and exploring the meaning of words in context	✓	✓	✓	✓	✓	✓	✓	✓	✓	✓	✓	✓	✓	✓	✓	✓	✓	✓	✓	✓
Asking questions to improve their understanding	✓	✓	✓	✓	✓	✓	✓	✓	✓	✓	✓	✓	✓	✓	✓	✓	✓	✓	✓	✓
Drawing inferences such as inferring characters' feelings, thoughts and motives from their actions, and justifying inferences with evidence	✓	✓	✓		✓	✓		✓	✓		✓		✓	✓		✓	✓	✓		
Predicting what might happen from details stated and implied		✓	✓					✓												
Summarising the main ideas drawn from more than one paragraph, identifying key details that support the main ideas			✓				✓								✓					
Identifying how language, structure and presentation contribute to meaning	✓	✓	✓			✓		✓		✓	✓	✓	✓	✓	✓	✓	✓		✓	✓
Discuss and evaluate how authors use language, including figurative language, considering the impact on the reader	✓	✓	✓		✓	✓	✓	✓	✓	✓	✓	✓	✓	✓	✓	✓	✓	✓	✓	✓
Distinguish between statements of fact and opinion				✓			✓					✓	✓		✓				✓	✓
Retrieve, record and present information from non-fiction				✓			✓						✓						✓	
Participate in discussions about books that are read to them and those they can read for themselves, building on their own and others' ideas and challenging views courteously	✓		✓	✓	✓	✓	✓	✓	✓	✓	✓	✓	✓	✓	✓	✓	✓	✓	✓	✓
Explain and discuss their understanding of what they have read, including through formal presentations and debates, maintaining a focus on the topic and using notes where necessary	✓	✓	✓	✓	✓	✓	✓	✓	✓	✓	✓	✓	✓	✓	✓	✓	✓	✓	✓	✓
Provide reasoned justifications for their views.	✓	✓	✓	✓	✓	✓	✓	✓	✓	✓	✓	✓	✓	✓	✓	✓	✓	✓	✓	✓

Treasure House resources overview

Unit	Title	Treasure House Resources	Collins Connect

1	Fiction: 'A Clever Way to Catch a Thief'	• Comprehension Skills Pupil Book 5, Unit 1, pages 4–6
		• Comprehension Skills Teacher's Guide 5
		  – Unit 1, pages 22–24
		  – Photocopiable Unit 1, Resource 1: Amy's character, page 85
		  – Photocopiable Unit 1, Resource 2: Servants' speech, page 86
			Collins Connect Treasure House Comprehension Year 5, Unit 1

2	Fiction: 'I Go Chicken-Dippy'	• Comprehension Skills Pupil Book 5, Unit 2, pages 7–9
		• Comprehension Skills Teacher's Guide 5
		  – Unit 2, pages 25–27
		  – Photocopiable Unit 2, Resource 1: Inside or outside?, page 87
		  – Photocopiable Unit 2, Resource 2: A dippy comic strip, page 88
			Collins Connect Treasure House Comprehension Year 5, Unit 2

3	Fiction (classic): 'Robinson Crusoe'	• Comprehension Skills Pupil Book 5, Unit 3, pages 10–12
		• Comprehension Skills Teacher's Guide 5
		  – Unit 3, pages 28–30
		  – Photocopiable Unit 3, Resource 1: Robinson Crusoe's character, page 89
		  – Photocopiable Unit 3, Resource 2: Other days' diaries, page 90
			Collins Connect Treasure House Comprehension Year 5, Unit 3

4	Non-fiction (news report): Cubs and Brownies to the rescue	• Comprehension Skills Pupil Book 5, Unit 4, pages 13–15
		• Comprehension Skills Teacher's Guide 5
		  – Unit 4, pages 31–33
		  – Photocopiable Unit 4, Resource 1: Finding the facts, page 91
		  – Photocopiable Unit 4, Resource 2: A new news report, page 92
			Collins Connect Treasure House Comprehension Year 5, Unit 4

5	Poetry: 'The Shark'	• Comprehension Skills Pupil Book 5, Unit 5, pages 16–18
		• Comprehension Skills Teacher's Guide 5
		  – Unit 5, pages 34–36
		  – Photocopiable Unit 5, Resource 1: My dangerous creature poem, page 93
		  – Photocopiable Unit 5, Resource 2: Shark facts, page 94
			Collins Connect Treasure House Comprehension Year 5, Unit 5

6	Poetry: 'Colonel Fazackerley'	• Comprehension Skills Pupil Book 5, Unit 6, pages 19–21
		• Comprehension Skills Teacher's Guide 5
		  – Unit 6, pages 37–39
		  – Photocopiable Unit 6, Resource 1: Getting the house to yourself, page 95
		  – Photocopiable Unit 6, Resource 2: Spectre storyboard, page 96
			Collins Connect Treasure House Comprehension Year 5, Unit 6

Unit	Title	Treasure House Resources	Collins Connect

7	Non-fiction (formal letter): 'Noisy neighbour'	• Comprehension Skills Pupil Book 5, Unit 7, pages 22–24
		• Comprehension Skills Teacher's Guide 5
		  – Unit 7, pages 40–42
		  – Photocopiable Unit 7, Resource 1: Three diaries, page 97
		  – Photocopiable Unit 7, Resource 2: A letter of complaint, page 98
			Collins Connect Treasure House Comprehension Year 5, Unit 7

8	Fiction (classic): 'The Borrowers'	• Comprehension Skills Pupil Book 5, Unit 8, pages 27–29
		• Comprehension Skills Teacher's Guide 5
		  – Unit 8, pages 44–46
		  – Photocopiable Unit 8, Resource 1: What the Borrowers took, page 99
		  – Photocopiable Unit 8, Resource 2: Kate's thoughts, page 100
			Collins Connect Treasure House Comprehension Year 5, Unit 8

9	Playscript: 'The Lost Gardens'	• Comprehension Skills Pupil Book 5, Unit 9, pages 30–32
		• Comprehension Skills Teacher's Guide 5
		  – Unit 9, pages 47–49
		  – Photocopiable Unit 9, Resource 1: Finding the features, page 101
		  – Photocopiable Unit 9, Resource 2: Different characters, page 102
			Collins Connect Treasure House Comprehension Year 5, Unit 9

10	Poetry: 'A Smuggler's Song'	• Comprehension Skills Pupil Book 5, Unit 10, pages 33–35
		• Comprehension Skills Teacher's Guide 5
		  – Unit 10, pages 50–52
		  – Photocopiable Unit 10, Resource 1: Smugglers page 103
		  – Photocopiable Unit 10, Resource 2: Good or bad?, page 104
			Collins Connect Treasure House Comprehension Year 5, Unit 10

11	Poetry: 'From a Railway Carriage'	• Comprehension Skills Pupil Book 5, Unit 11, pages 36–38
		• Comprehension Skills Teacher's Guide 5
		  – Unit 11, pages 53–55
		  – Photocopiable Unit 11, Resource 1: Finding the beat, page 105
		  – Photocopiable Unit 11, Resource 2: A mind map, page 106
			Collins Connect Treasure House Comprehension Year 5, Unit 11

12	Non-fiction (instructions): 'Magic matchsticks'	• Comprehension Skills Pupil Book 5, Unit 12, pages 39–41
		• Comprehension Skills Teacher's Guide 5
		  – Unit 12, pages 56–58
		  – Photocopiable Unit 12, Resource 1: Making a cup of tea, page 107
		  – Photocopiable Unit 12, Resource 2: Writing a recipe, page 108
			Collins Connect Treasure House Comprehension Year 5, Unit 12

Unit	Title	Treasure House Resources	Collins Connect

13	Non-fiction (historical): 'The Trojan War'	• Comprehension Skills Pupil Book 5, Unit 13, pages 42–44
		• Comprehension Skills Teacher's Guide 5
		  – Unit 13, pages 59–61
		  – Photocopiable Unit 13, Resource 1: Quick quiz, page 109
		  – Photocopiable Unit 13, Resource 2: A Trojan comic strip, page 110
			Collins Connect Treasure House Comprehension Year 5, Unit 13

14	Fiction (legend): 'Shen Nung'	• Comprehension Skills Pupil Book 5, Unit 14, pages 45–47
		• Comprehension Skills Teacher's Guide 5
		  – Unit 14, pages 62–64
		  – Photocopiable Unit 14, Resource 1: Shen Nung's character, page 111
		  – Photocopiable Unit 14, Resource 2: An important discovery, page 112
			Collins Connect Treasure House Comprehension Year 5, Unit 14

15	Non-fiction (biography): 'Barack Obama'	• Comprehension Skills Pupil Book 5, Unit 15, pages 50–52
		• Comprehension Skills Teacher's Guide 5
		  – Unit 15, pages 66–68
		  – Photocopiable Unit 15, Resource 1: Questions about the USA, page 113
		  – Photocopiable Unit 15, Resource 2: Researching civil rights, page 114
			Collins Connect Treasure House Comprehension Year 5, Unit 15

16	Fiction (modern): 'The Hedgehog Mystery'	• Comprehension Skills Pupil Book 5, Unit 16, pages 53–55
		• Comprehension Skills Teacher's Guide 5
		  – Unit 16, pages 69–71
		  – Photocopiable Unit 16, Resource 1: Mum and Gran, page 115
		  – Photocopiable Unit 16, Resource 2: Gang rules, page 116	

17	Fiction (traditional tale): 'The Dragon Pearl'	• Comprehension Skills Pupil Book 5, Unit 17, pages 56–58
		• Comprehension Skills Teacher's Guide 5
		  – Unit 17, pages 72–74
		  – Photocopiable Unit 17, Resource 1: The magical pearl, page 117
		  – Photocopiable Unit 17, Resource 2: The start of the story, page 118	

18	Poetry: 'What on Earth?' and 'Progress Man'	• Comprehension Skills Pupil Book 5, Unit 18, pages 59–61
		• Comprehension Skills Teacher's Guide 5
		  – Unit 18, pages 75–77
		  – Photocopiable Unit 18, Resource 1: Comparing the poems, page 119
		  – Photocopiable Unit 18, Resource 2: My progress poem, page 120	

Unit	Title	Treasure House Resources	Collins Connect

19	Non-fiction (information text): 'How to be an Ancient Greek in 25 easy stages'	• Comprehension Skills Pupil Book 5, Unit 19, pages 62–64
		• Comprehension Skills Teacher's Guide 5
		  – Unit 19, pages 78–80
		  – Photocopiable Unit 19, Resource 1: Quick quiz, page 121
		  – Photocopiable Unit 19, Resource 2: Ancient instructions, page 122	

20	Non-fiction (autobiography): 'Ade Adepitan: A Paralympian's Story'	• Comprehension Skills Pupil Book 5, Unit 20, pages 65–67
		• Comprehension Skills Teacher's Guide 5
		  – Unit 20, pages 81–83
		  – Photocopiable Unit 20, Resource 1: Ade's reasons, page 123
		  – Photocopiable Unit 20, Resource 2: Fact or opinion?, page 124	

Unit 1: Fiction: 'A Clever Way to Catch a Thief'

Overview

English curriculum objectives

- Continue to read and discuss an increasingly wide range of fiction, poetry, plays, non-fiction and reference books or textbooks
- Increase their familiarity with a wide range of books, including myths, legends and traditional stories, modern fiction, fiction from our literary heritage, and books from other cultures and traditions
- Recommend books that they have read to their peers, giving reasons for their choices
- Identify and discuss themes and conventions in and across a wide range of writing
- Make comparisons within and across books
- Check that the book makes sense to them, discussing their understanding and exploring the meaning of words in context
- Ask questions to improve their understanding
- Draw inferences such as inferring characters' feelings, thoughts and motives from their actions, and justifying inferences with evidence
- Predict what might happen from details stated and implied
- Identify how language, structure and presentation contribute to meaning
- Discuss and evaluate how authors use language, including figurative language, considering the impact on the reader
- Participate in discussions about books that are read to them and those they can read for themselves, building on their own and others' ideas and challenging views courteously
- Explain and discuss their understanding of what they have read, including through formal presentations and debates, maintaining a focus on the topic and using notes where necessary
- Provide reasoned justification for their views

Treasure House resources

- Comprehension Skills Pupil Book 5, Unit 1, pages 4–6
- Collins Connect Treasure House Comprehension Year 5, Unit 1
- Photocopiable Unit 1, Resource 1: How the thief was caught, page 85
- Photocopiable Unit 1, Resource 2: Servants' speech, page 86

Additional resources

- Dictionaries or the internet
- Other mystery stories, such as *Ruby Redfort: Look into My Eyes* by Lauren Child (optional)

Introduction

Teaching overview

A Clever Way to Catch a Thief is a short story about a man who devises a trick to reveal which servant has been stealing from him. Like the suspects in the story, the reader learns about the true nature of the trap only after it has been used and the thief caught. The story encourages children to draw inferences regarding characters' feelings, thoughts and motives from their actions, and to justify inferences with evidence. There are opportunities to develop children's ability to evaluate how authors use language to portray characters' feelings, thoughts and motives, considering the impact on the reader.

Introduce the story

Ask the children if any of them have read any mystery stories, and invite them to share their experiences and knowledge of mystery stories' characteristics with the class.

Tell the children that, in this lesson, they will focus on a short mystery story. Then they will answer questions about it. Remind children that sometimes the answers to the questions will be clearly written in the story, but that sometimes they may need to think a little harder and use their own ideas, supported by the text.

Ask the children to read the story individually or in pairs. Ask them to note down any words they do not understand. Discuss unknown or unusual vocabulary before setting children to work answering the questions in the Pupil Book. Try to avoid discussing the content of the story until after the children have answered the questions.

Unit 1: Fiction: 'A Clever Way to Catch a Thief'

Pupil practice

Pupil Book pages 4–6

Get started

Ask children to write sentences to answer the questions, referring to the text where possible.

Suggested answers

1. When the servants were 'perplexed' they were very confused. When the rich man wanted to prove a servant's 'guilt' he wanted to prove someone had done something wrong. Most of the servants wanted to prove their 'innocence', meaning the fact that they had done nothing wrong. When the servants were 'anxious' they were worried. There was a black powder called 'soot', which is made by a fire's smoke, on the box. [5 marks]
2. The rich man thought one of his servants had been stealing from him because he was constantly losing things from his house. [1 mark]
3. The innocent servants had nothing to fear because the rich man said the cockerel would detect their innocence and not crow. [1 mark]
4. The innocent servants had soot on their hands. [1 mark]
5. There was no cockerel, so it could not make a sound. [1 mark]
6. The event in the text happened one evening, as it was getting dark. [1 mark]
7. The rich man wanted to check the servants' left hands. [1 mark]
8. The rich man knew who the guilty servant was because there was no soot on his/her hand. [1 mark]

Try these

Ask children to write sentences to answer the questions, explaining their answers as fully as they can. The children's answers may be subjective but should be in their own words and well justified, using evidence from either the text or the children's own experiences.

Possible answers

1. Answers should suggest that the rich man felt sad, betrayed and/or disappointed when he realised someone was stealing from him, because he wanted to trust his servants. [2 marks]
2. Answers should suggest that the servants were 'sorry to think that one of their number was untrustworthy' because they wanted to trust each other and keep the rich man's trust. [2 marks]
3. Answers should recognise that the rich man pretended he had a magical cockerel in order to trick the guilty servant into revealing himself/herself. [2 marks]
4. Answers could conclude that the innocent servants may have felt confidence that they were innocent / worry that the cockerel would mistake them for guilty / disbelief in the rich man's trick when they were going into the dark room. [2 marks]
5. Answers should conclude that the guilty servant may have felt fear of being caught and/or confident that he or she could outsmart the rich man when he or she was going into the dark room. [2 marks]
6. Answers could suggest that some of the servants thought the rich man was going mad because they did not believe in magic and so thought his plan was ridiculous. [2 marks]
7. Answers could suggest that the rich man may sack the guilty servant / turn the guilty servant over to the police / try to get his stolen things back / punish the guilty servant. [2 marks]
8. Answers could conclude that the story is historical as it is referred to as an 'old tale' and contains references to servants, soot and magic, or that it is not historical as everything in it still exists today. [2 marks]

Now try these

The children's answers will be subjective, but should be well justified where appropriate.

Possible answers

1. Answers could refer to the thief's initial motives for the theft, fear of being caught, attempt to trick the cockerel and reaction to being proved guilty. [3 marks max]
2. Answers could refer to the rich man's cleverness, trickery or reassuring treatment of the innocent servants. [3 marks max]
3. Answers should recognise that, from this moment, the rich man begins to reveal his real plan and proceeds to expose the thief. [3 marks max]
4. Answers should recognise that this phrase describes the rich man accusing the thief, and that the word 'thrusting' describes a quick and assertive movement. This is effective as it conveys the emotion felt by the rich man towards the thief: anger and/or pride at his trick working. [3 marks max]
5. Open-ended question: Look for relevance to the plot and characters established, and correct punctuation of dialogue. The story's moral could refer to stealing/lying being wrong, and should acknowledge that it was the thief's attempt to avoid the cockerel's judgement that proved his or her guilt. [3 marks max]

Unit 1: Fiction: 'A Clever Way to Catch a Thief'

Support, embed & challenge

Support
Use Unit 1 Resource 1: How the thief was caught to support children in clarifying the rich man's plan and how the thief reacted to it. Ask them to answer each of the questions as though they are the thief.

Embed
Use Unit 1 Resource 2: Servants' speech to encourage children to consider how the servants may have reacted to hearing the rich man's plan. Children should write dialogue that discusses the plan before it is carried out, thinking about the servants' point of view throughout.

Challenge
Challenge children to rewrite the story as a playscript, remembering to include stage directions. They could also make notes about the set they would like to use, and costumes for the characters.

Homework / Additional activities

A modern mystery
Ask children to write their own story using a similar storyline, but modernised rather than historical. Ask them to think about what situation they will use (perhaps a school setting) and what details they will need to change to bring the story into modern times.

Collins Connect: Unit 1
Ask the children to complete Unit 1 (see Teach → Year 5 → Comprehension → Unit 1).

Unit 2: Fiction: 'I Go Chicken-Dippy'

Overview

English curriculum objectives

- Continue to read and discuss an increasingly wide range of fiction, poetry, plays, non-fiction and reference books or textbooks
- Increase their familiarity with a wide range of books, including myths, legends and traditional stories, modern fiction, fiction from our literary heritage, and books from other cultures and traditions
- Recommend books that they have read to their peers, giving reasons for their choices
- Identify and discuss themes and conventions in and across a wide range of writing
- Make comparisons within and across books
- Check that the book makes sense to them, discussing their understanding and exploring the meaning of words in context
- Ask questions to improve their understanding
- Draw inferences such as inferring characters' feelings, thoughts and motives from their actions, and justifying inferences with evidence
- Predict what might happen from details stated and implied
- Identify how language, structure and presentation contribute to meaning
- Discuss and evaluate how authors use language, including figurative language, considering the impact on the reader
- Participate in discussions about books that are read to them and those they can read for themselves, building on their own and others' ideas and challenging views courteously
- Explain and discuss their understanding of what they have read, including through formal presentations and debates, maintaining a focus on the topic and using notes where necessary
- Provide reasoned justification for their views

Treasure House resources

- Comprehension Skills Pupil Book 5, Unit 2, pages 7–9
- Collins Connect Treasure House Comprehension Year 5, Unit 2
- Photocopiable Unit 2, Resource 1: Inside or outside? page 87
- Photocopiable Unit 2, Resource 2: A dippy comic strip, page 88

Additional resources

- Dictionaries or the internet
- *The Chicken Gave It to Me* by Anne Fine, whole text (optional)

Introduction

Teaching overview

'I Go Chicken-Dippy' is an extract from Anne Fine's book *The Chicken Gave It to Me*. This tells the story of two children who discover a dirty old book in which a chicken has told 'The True Story of Harrowing Farm', a farm near the children's school, explaining how badly the chickens were treated. In 'I Go Chicken-Dippy' the chicken recalls her first moments of freedom outside her cage.

Introduce the extract

Ask the children if they know the story *The Chicken Gave It To Me*. If they do, invite them to share their knowledge with the class. Then ask them if they know anything about the difference between battery chicken farming and free-range chicken farming. Again, ask them to share their knowledge.

Tell the children that, in this lesson, they will focus on an extract from a story in which a battery-farmed chicken first experiences the outside world. Then they will answer questions about it. Remind children that sometimes the answers to the questions will be clearly written in the extract, but that sometimes they may need to think a little harder and use their own ideas, supported by the text.

Ask the children to read the extract individually or in pairs. Ask them to note down any words they do not understand. Discuss unknown or unusual vocabulary before setting children to work answering the questions in the Pupil Book. Try to avoid discussing the content of the extract until after the children have answered the questions.

Unit 2: Fiction: 'I Go Chicken-Dippy'

Pupil practice

Pupil Book pages 7–9

Get started

Ask children to write sentences to answer the questions, referring to the text where possible.

Suggested answers

1. The chicken had never been outside before. [1 mark]
2. The first thing the chicken felt outside was the wet air and wind. [1 mark]
3. The wet air ruffled the chicken's feathers. [1 mark]
4. The chicken was staggering about in a slimy mud puddle. [1 mark]
5. The temperature outside was cold. [1 mark]
6. The chicken could hear roaring wind and creaking treetops. [1 mark]
7. The chicken shed was cleaned out during the week, but not at weekends. [1 mark]
8. The workers wore masks and had red-rimmed eyes. [1 mark]

Try these

Ask children to write sentences to answer the questions, explaining their answers as fully as they can. The children's answers may be subjective but should be in their own words and well justified, using evidence from either the text or the children's own experiences.

Possible answers

1. Answers should recognise that the chicken would prefer to be outside in the storm, as it was excited at feeling new things and did not like the poor conditions in the shed. [2 marks]
2. Answers should conclude that there was a terrible smell and possible health risks in the shed. [2 marks]
3. Answers should recognise that the chicken lacked experience and knowledge of the things it was smelling. [2 marks]
4. Answers should recognise that the chicken had never been outside before as it had been confined in the shed. They could also refer to battery farming. [2 marks]
5. Answers should recognise that the chicken felt it 'couldn't handle it all' as it was experiencing lots of different new sensations, but should not suggest that these made the chicken unhappy or keen to return to the shed. [2 marks]
6. Answers should conclude that 'chicken-dippy' refers to the sense of crazy joy that the chicken was experiencing. [2 marks]
7. Answers should recognise that it is cheaper to keep chickens in crowded sheds as they are easily controlled, fit in more chickens and require fewer workers. [2 marks]
8. Answers could refer to the chickens' wellbeing and/or to the need for farmers to make money. [2 marks]

Now try these

The children's answers will be subjective, but should be well justified where appropriate.

Possible answers

1. Answers could refer to the chicken's enthusiasm, joy, previous suffering and/or ignorance of the world. [3 marks max]
2. Mind maps could refer to the chicken's initial discomfort, routine and its surprise at being outside, and then should refer to the emotions mentioned in the extract. [3 marks max]
3. The author used senses of touch, sound, sight and smell. Answers should recognise that this builds up a vivid picture for the reader. [3 marks max]
4. Answers could conclude that the short fragments create a sense of the speed of impressions on the chicken, and/or the chicken's 'dippy' state of mind. [3 marks max]
5. Open-ended question: Look for relevance to the plot and character established, and for clear and atmospheric descriptions of different senses. [3 marks max]

Support, embed & challenge

Support

Use Unit 2 Resource 1: Inside or outside? to support children in paying close attention to the detail of the descriptions of setting in the extract. Ask them to reread the text and to fill in the table as they read.

Embed

Use Unit 2 Resource 2: A dippy comic strip to encourage children to explore the plot of the story. Ask children to retell the story using a comic strip layout and style. Support them in thinking about how they will divide the story into the number of boxes given in the comic strip template, and how they will use the thought and speech bubbles. Support children in summarising each scene to retell the story using minimal words.

Challenge

Challenge children to think carefully about the theme of the story. Ask them to write their own short story based on the theme of acquiring freedom, but using human characters instead of animals. Ask: 'What might your main character experience and learn during your story?'

Unit 2: Fiction: 'I Go Chicken-Dippy'

Homework / Additional activities

Farming facts
Ask the children to research other issues that affect farming. The children could also be asked to present or share the information they find with small groups or the whole class.

Collins Connect: Unit 2
Ask the children to complete Unit 2 (see Teach → Year 5 → Comprehension → Unit 2).

Unit 3: Fiction (classic): 'Robinson Crusoe'

Overview

English curriculum objectives

- Continue to read and discuss an increasingly wide range of fiction, poetry, plays, non-fiction and reference books or textbooks
- Increase their familiarity with a wide range of books, including myths, legends and traditional stories, modern fiction, fiction from our literary heritage, and books from other cultures and traditions
- Recommend books that they have read to their peers, giving reasons for their choices
- Identify and discuss themes and conventions in and across a wide range of writing
- Make comparisons within and across books
- Check that the book makes sense to them, discussing their understanding and exploring the meaning of words in context
- Ask questions to improve their understanding
- Draw inferences such as inferring characters' feelings, thoughts and motives from their actions, and justifying inferences with evidence
- Predict what might happen from details stated and implied
- Identify how language, structure and presentation contribute to meaning
- Discuss and evaluate how authors use language, including figurative language, considering the impact on the reader
- Participate in discussions about books that are read to them and those they can read for themselves, building on their own and others' ideas and challenging views courteously
- Explain and discuss their understanding of what they have read, including through formal presentations and debates, maintaining a focus on the topic and using notes where necessary
- Provide reasoned justification for their views

Treasure House resources

- Comprehension Skills Pupil Book 5, Unit 3, pages 10–12
- Collins Connect Treasure House Comprehension Year 5, Unit 3
- Photocopiable Unit 3, Resource 1: Robinson Crusoe's character, page 89
- Photocopiable Unit 3, Resource 2: Other days' diaries, page 90

Additional resources

- Dictionaries or the internet
- *Robinson Crusoe* by Daniel Defoe, whole text (optional)

Introduction

Teaching overview

Robinson Crusoe is a novel written by Daniel Defoe, first published in 1719. The story is presented as an autobiography of a castaway who spent 30 years living on a remote tropical island after being shipwrecked. The extract describes Crusoe's early days on the island and is written from his perspective.

Introduce the extract

Ask the children if any of them know the story *Robinson Crusoe*. If they do, invite them to share their knowledge with the class.

Relate the information given in the 'Teaching overview' above, and tell the children that, in this lesson, they will focus on one extract from this diary-style narrative. Then they will answer questions about it. Remind children that sometimes the answers to the questions will be clearly written in the extract, but that sometimes they may need to think a little harder and use their own ideas, supported by the text.

Ask the children to read the extract individually or in pairs. Ask them to note down any words they do not understand. Discuss unknown or unusual vocabulary before setting children to work answering the questions in the Pupil Book. Try to avoid discussing the content of the extract until after the children have answered the questions.

Pupil practice

Pupil Book pages 10–12

Get started
Ask children to write sentences to answer the questions, referring to the text where possible.

Suggested answers

1. Robinson Crusoe has been shipwrecked for eight days. [1 mark]
2. On the eighth day, Crusoe was surprised to see Japp the dog. [1 mark]
3. Japp was an Irish setter. [1 mark]
4. Japp had belonged to the ship's captain. [1 mark]
5. Crusoe thought it had been difficult for Japp to find him because Japp may have been swept away by the current and landed much further away on the island. [1 mark]
6. Crusoe built a tent with the poles and sail-cloth. [1 mark]
7. Crusoe ate dried meat and a ship's biscuit for dinner. [1 mark]
8. Crusoe recovered a quantity of tools, a drill, a dozen hatchets, a grind-stone for sharpening, iron crowbars, a large bag of nails and rivets, sails, ropes, poles, two barrels of powder, a box of musket balls, seven muskets, a third shotgun, lead, a hammock, a mattress, blankets, clothes, great coats, dried meat, biscuits and Japp the dog. (Answers should list any five of these items.) [5 marks]

Try these
Ask children to write sentences to answer the questions, explaining their answers as fully as they can. The children's answers may be subjective but should be in their own words and well justified, using evidence from either the text or the children's own experiences.

Possible answers

1. Answers should recognise that the accident almost cost Crusoe his life. They should also conclude that he is afraid of dying on the island (specifically, of drowning) as all his crewmates did in the shipwreck. [2 marks]
2. Answers should state that Japp was happy to see Crusoe, as he was 'bounding joyfully' towards him. [2 marks]
3. Answers could suggest that Crusoe was sympathetic to the dog (calling him 'poor beast'), that Crusoe soon called Japp 'my dog' and/or that he slept with Japp at his feet. [2 marks]
4. Answers should refer to Crusoe's apparent contentment and his expectation of 'a good night'. [2 marks]
5. Answers should detect that Crusoe ate so little as he was rationing himself due to a lack of food on the island. [2 marks]
6. Answers should conclude that Crusoe will use the tools to assist in his survival and/or escape. [2 marks]
7. Answers could detect that Crusoe is recording facts and actions rather than feelings, and could suggest that he wants to keep busy and/or keep track of time. [2 marks]
8. Answers should relate clues that this is a historical story, such as references to great coats, barrels of powder, muskets and musket balls, as well as the wider context of expeditions on large-scale sailing ships of this type. [2 marks]

Now try these
The children's answers will be subjective, but should be well justified where appropriate.

Possible answers

1. Answers could refer to Crusoe being practical and hardworking, his fondness for the dog and/or apparent lack of emotion. [3 marks max]
2. Mind maps could refer to Crusoe's initial enjoyment of the voyage, his fear during the shipwreck, his survival on the island and his eventual plans. [3 marks max]
3. Answers could include the inclusion of the date, the use of the first person, the past tense (mostly), the informal and conversational tone, the close descriptions and the inclusion of hopes for the future. [3 marks max]
4. Crusoe returned to the wreck, capsized in the creek and found Japp. Answers could refer to Crusoe describing his thoughts (his stream of consciousness) and using detailed descriptions, rather than trying to convey quick actions, and could add that it creates the effect of Crusoe having a great deal of time (and little else) at his disposal. [3 marks max]
5. Open-ended question: Look for relevance to the plot and character established, and for sensitivity about what Crusoe tells his family (that is, he could try to give his location but may not describe the horror of the wreck). [3 marks max]

Unit 3: Fiction (classic): 'Robinson Crusoe'

Support, embed & challenge

Support
Use Unit 3 Resource 1: Robinson Crusoe's character to support children in exploring the character of Robinson Crusoe further. Children should reread the text carefully to extract information that they can use in the profile. If the information isn't easily located in the extract, discuss with the children what the answers could be, encouraging them to infer ideas from the text and expand their own thoughts about Crusoe.

Embed
Use Unit 3 Resource 2: Other days' diaries to encourage children to think about how Crusoe would think, behave and feel at different points by asking them to write two more diary entries from his point of view: of the day the shipwreck happened and of the day after that described in the extract.

Challenge
Challenge children to improvise a film trailer for a cinematic adaptation of *Robinson Crusoe*. Ask: 'What focus will the film and trailer have? Will you show a dramatic scene, such as the shipwreck, or a more personal depiction of Crusoe himself?' Ask children to create a storyboard for their trailer, and also to write it as a playscript.

Homework / Additional activities

What happens next?
Ask children to research and find out how the story of *Robinson Crusoe* concludes, providing an adaptation of the full text if possible.

Collins Connect: Unit 3
Ask the children to complete Unit 3 (see Teach → Year 5 → Comprehension → Unit 3).

Unit 4: Non-fiction (news report): 'Cubs and Brownies to the rescue'

Overview

English curriculum objectives

- Continue to read and discuss an increasingly wide range of fiction, poetry, plays, non-fiction and reference books or textbooks
- Read books that are structured in different ways and read for a range of purposes
- Identify and discuss themes and conventions in and across a wide range of writing
- Check that the book makes sense to them, discussing their understanding and exploring the meaning of words in context
- Ask questions to improve their understanding
- Summarise the main ideas drawn from more than one paragraph, identifying key details that support the main idea
- Identify how language, structure and presentation contribute to meaning
- Distinguish between statements of fact and opinion
- Retrieve, record and present information from non-fiction
- Participate in discussions about books that are read to them and those they can read for themselves, building on their own and others' ideas and challenging views courteously
- Explain and discuss their understanding of what they have read, including through formal presentations and debates, maintaining a focus on the topic and using notes where necessary
- Provide reasoned justification for their views

Treasure House resources

- Comprehension Skills Pupil Book 5, Unit 4, pages 13–15
- Collins Connect Treasure House Comprehension Year 5, Unit 4
- Photocopiable Unit 4, Resource 1: Finding the facts, page 91
- Photocopiable Unit 4, Resource 2: A new news report, page 92

Additional resources

- Dictionaries or the internet
- Other examples of local news stories (optional)

Introduction

Teaching overview

'Cubs and Brownies to the rescue' is an example of a local good-news story that details a community coming together to clean up their local area. Through this article children are able to observe and utilise characteristics common to news reports, such as headlines, by-lines, quotes, captioned images, summary introductions (explaining who, what, when and where) and body text (further explaining how and why).

Introduce the text

Ask the children what they know about the features, purpose and audience of newspaper reports. Ask them to share their knowledge with the class.

Tell the children that, in this lesson, they will focus on a news report about a community event. Then they will answer questions about it. Remind children that sometimes the answers to the questions will be clearly written in the report, but that sometimes they may need to think a little harder and use their own ideas, supported by the text.

Ask the children to read the report individually or in pairs. Ask them to note down any words they do not understand. Discuss unknown or unusual vocabulary before setting children to work answering the questions in the Pupil Book. Try to avoid discussing the content of the report until after the children have answered the questions.

Unit 4: Non-fiction (news report): 'Cubs and Brownies to the rescue'

Pupil practice

Pupil Book pages 13–15

Get started

Ask children to write sentences to answer the questions, referring to the text where possible.

Suggested answers

1. An 'angler' is someone who might fish in the river that the RESCUE event is cleaning. A group that is 'voluntary' might offer to help with the RESCUE event without any payment. The RESCUE 'scheme' is a plan of what the RESCUE team might do. The scheme being 'launched' means it was started. The clean-up was removing 'refuse', which means rubbish. If someone 'disposes' of something in the park, it means they throw it away there. [6 marks]
2. The people involved in the event were the Brownies, the Cubs, anglers, conservation volunteers, Moreton Town Council, Friends of Caversham Woods, and other local authorities and voluntary groups. [1 mark]
3. The clean-up happens once a year ('annually'). [1 mark]
4. The clean-up happened on 3 August. [1 mark]
5. The scheme was launched three years ago. [1 mark]
6. There was twice the volume of rubbish in the first year as in the current year. [1 mark]
7. A few local residents are still dumping garden refuse in the park. [1 mark]
8. It was wrong to leave engine oil in a litter bin as it is illegal and it may cause a pollution accident. [1 mark]

Try these

Ask children to write sentences to answer the questions, explaining their answers as fully as they can. The children's answers may be subjective but should be in their own words and well justified, using evidence from either the text or the children's own experiences.

Possible answers

1. Answers could suggest that Cubs and Brownies were helping with the clean-up because they cared about the environment and/or because they were working towards badges. [2 marks]
2. Answers could suggest that Cubs and Brownies may have felt proud about helping and/or disappointed about all the rubbish and the harm to the environment people are causing. [2 marks]
3. Answers could suggest that someone might dump rubbish in a park due to laziness, because they don't care about the environment and/or because of a lack of proper refuse facilities. [2 marks]
4. Answers could suggest that the rubbish looks and smells bad, causes environmental pollution and/or poses a danger to wildlife. [2 marks]
5. Answers should detect that the spokeswoman for the environment department seemed disappointed/angry with residents who dump refuse in the park. [2 marks]
6. Answers should conclude that the main feeling the mayor expressed was that he was pleased to see so many young people helping to clean up the park. [2 marks]
7. Answers could suggest that readers may be interested in a local park, the environment and/or the Cubs and/or Brownies. [2 marks]
8. Answers could conclude that the report might have a positive or negative effect on the people who dump rubbish in the park as it may spread awareness of the problem (causing fewer people to leave rubbish) or allow them to believe that others will clear up their mess (causing an increase in the amount of rubbish left). [2 marks]

Now try these

The children's answers will be subjective, but should be well justified where appropriate.

Possible answers

1. Answers should recognise that the RESCUE event extends beyond the clean-up of the park. The report suggests it also involves environmental work in the local woods and rivers. [3 marks max]
2. The three features listed could include headlines, by-lines, quotes, captioned images, summary introductions (explaining who, what, when and where) and body text (further explaining how and why). [3 marks max]
3. Answers should conclude that the quotations give opinions about the issue and event, and that these opinions contrast with one another. They could add that the quotations make the report more personal and show the effects of the event on the community. [3 marks max]
4. Open-ended question: Look for relevance to the topic and event reported, presentation and creativity. The leaflets or posters should include information like the illegality of leaving engine oil in bins and the risks of pollution. [3 marks max]
5. Open-ended question: Look for relevance to the topic and event, and the mayor's positive attitude. The speeches should use appropriately formal language. [3 marks max]

Support, embed & challenge

Support
Use Unit 4 Resource 1: Finding the facts to support children in extracting the facts from the newspaper report. Read through the chart and discuss where each piece of information is in the report. Discuss the difference between 'why' and 'how': 'why' asks for reasons and motivations, whereas 'how' asks for a description of the manner in which an event occurred.

Embed
Use Unit 4 Resource 2: A new news report to encourage children to think more about the features of news reports, and about events after the big clean-up. Ask children to imagine that someone dumps a van-load of refuse in the park the very next day. Ask them to write a news report about this, referring to the extract for information and ideas.

Challenge
Challenge children to create a plan of how their school could improve the school grounds with regard to littering and recycling. You could encourage them to do some further research to discover what other schools do for this cause.

Homework / Additional activities

Real rubbish rescues
Ask children to carry out some research about local council initiatives to keep the area litter free. Ask them to be prepared to discuss their findings with a group or the class.

Collins Connect: Unit 4
Ask the children to complete Unit 4 (see Teach → Year 5 → Comprehension → Unit 4).

Unit 5: Poetry: 'The Shark'

Overview

English curriculum objectives
- Continue to read and discuss an increasingly wide range of fiction, poetry, plays, non-fiction and reference books or textbooks
- Identify and discuss themes and conventions in and across a wide range of writing
- Learn a wider range of poetry by heart
- Prepare poems and plays to read aloud and to perform, showing understanding through intonation, tone and volume so that the meaning is clear to an audience
- Check that the book makes sense to them, discussing their understanding and exploring the meaning of words in context
- Ask questions to improve their understanding
- Draw inferences such as inferring characters' feelings, thoughts and motives from their actions, and justifying inferences with evidence
- Identify how language, structure and presentation contribute to meaning
- Discuss and evaluate how authors use language, including figurative language, considering the impact on the reader
- Participate in discussions about books that are read to them and those they can read for themselves, building on their own and others' ideas and challenging views courteously
- Explain and discuss their understanding of what they have read, including through formal presentations and debates, maintaining a focus on the topic and using notes where necessary
- Provide reasoned justification for their views

Treasure House resources
- Comprehension Skills Pupil Book 5, Unit 5, pages 16–18
- Collins Connect Treasure House Comprehension Year 5, Unit 5
- Photocopiable Unit 5, Resource 1: My dangerous creature poem, page 93
- Photocopiable Unit 5, Resource 2: Shark facts, page 94

Additional resources
- Dictionaries or the internet
- Non-fiction texts about sharks

Introduction

Teaching overview
'The Shark', written by Lord Alfred Douglas in the late 1800s, is an example of a poem that observes the power and mystery of a dangerous animal. The speaker in the poem details the characteristics and behaviour of the shark with cautious wonder and awe, rather than revulsion or hostility. There are opportunities to develop children's ability to evaluate how authors use poetic language to portray characters' feelings, thoughts and motives, considering the impact on the reader.

Introduce the poem
Ask the children what they know about sharks, and invite them to share their knowledge with the class. Scribe descriptions of sharks' appearance and characteristics on the board as the children suggest them.

Tell the children that, in this lesson, they will focus on a poem about a shark. Then they will answer questions about it. Remind children that sometimes the answers to the questions will be clearly written in the poem, but that sometimes they may need to think a little harder and use their own ideas, supported by the text.

Ask the children to read the poem individually or in pairs. Ask them to note down any words they do not understand. Discuss unknown or unusual vocabulary before setting children to work answering the questions in the Pupil Book. Try to avoid discussing the content of the poem until after the children have answered the questions.

Unit 5: Poetry: 'The Shark'

Pupil practice

Pupil Book pages 16–18

Get started

Ask children to write sentences to answer the questions, referring to the text where possible.

Suggested answers

1. The poet thinks the shark's self-control is 'astounding', which means he is very surprised and impressed by it. The shark's 'range' is the distance within which he can attack. The shark's 'demeanour' is his mood and outward behaviour. When the shark shows his true 'character', he shows his true nature and qualities. If you were 'appealing' to the shark, you would be asking for help or mercy. [5 marks max]

2. The poet says the shark's eyes 'do not grow bright or roll'. [1 mark]

3. The shark does not seem to want to land 'when he sees you on the sand'. [1 mark]

4. The shark does not show any excitement 'when he watches you take off your clothes'. [1 mark]

5. When his demeanour changes, the shark throws his body right about. [1 mark]

6. No, the shark's behaviour doesn't change when you first get into the sea. [1 mark]

7. The shark's behaviour changes when you get into his range. [1 mark]

8. After reading the poem, the poet believes the reader will wish to keep clear of sharks. [1 mark]

Try these

Ask children to write sentences to answer the questions, explaining their answers as fully as they can. The children's answers may be subjective but should be in their own words and well justified, using evidence from either the text or the children's own experiences.

Possible answers

1. Answers should recognise that the word 'monster' creates negative feelings towards the shark, perhaps likening it to dangerous fictional beasts. [2 marks]

2. Answers should state that the meaning of the word 'treacherous' is related to betrayal or unpredictability. They could expand that this relates to the contrast between the way the shark seems to act and its 'true nature'. [2 marks]

3. Answers should conclude that the shark's 'true character' is violent and dangerous. [2 marks]

4. Answers could suggest that the shark might pretend 'to take no interest' until you 'get in his range' as it does not wish to draw attention to itself and/or to scare away prey. [2 marks]

5. Answers could note that rhyming couplets have potential for humour and light-heartedness, and help to make the poem's attitude seem positive. [2 marks]

6. Answers should recognise that the poet shows a fascination with the shark, and an admiration of the shark's ability to control itself. [2 marks]

7. Answers should recognise that having 'decent feeling' requires both feeling/emotion and a sense of decency or good behaviour. They could suggest that animals do have feelings and can learn to recognise good behaviour, or that they do not have feelings or knowledge similar enough to humans to generate a sense of decency. [2 marks]

8. The two things the poet writes about the shark that usually only apply to people are 'He never makes the least remark' and 'He looks as if he were asleep'. [2 marks]

Now try these

The children's answers will be subjective, but should be well justified where appropriate.

Possible answers

1. Answers could refer to the shark's apparent patience, treacherousness, violence and dangerous nature. [3 marks]

2. Rhyming couplets should be from the shark's point of view and be consistent with its character as detailed by the poem. [3 marks]

3. Answers should recognise that the line that starts with 'But' is a turning point in the poem because, from this moment, the poet describes the shark's 'true character'. [3 marks max]

4. Answers should recognise that this is the only phrase that describes how the shark moves. They could note that the rest of the poem describes the shark's lack of movement, and its nature. [3 marks max]

5. Open-ended question: Look for relevance to the situation and perspective of the character established, and a poetic form similar to that of the poem. [3 marks max]

Unit 5: Poetry: 'The Shark'

Support, embed & challenge

Support
Support children in examining the information in the poem by supplying copies for them to annotate. Ask them to highlight any information they think is a fact in one colour, opinions in another and anything they think may be untrue in a third colour.

Embed
Use Unit 5 Resource 1: My dangerous creature poem to encourage children to plan their own poem about a dangerous animal. Ask children to think carefully about the rhymes they will use, and the language they will choose to portray the chosen animal's different behaviours and characteristics. Suggest to the children that they consider describing the animal in words that are more usually used to describe people.

Challenge
Challenge children to use Unit 5 Resource 2: Shark facts to structure research about sharks in non-fiction texts. Encourage them to find the most unusual facts they can. Then ask them to discuss whether or not they think the content of the poem is accurate, based on their research findings.

Homework / Additional activities

Animal behaviours
Ask children to make notes about humorous things that other animals do. They could use their pets for inspiration, or choose an animal they like.

Collins Connect: Unit 5
Ask the children to complete Unit 5 (see Teach → Year 5 → Comprehension → Unit 5).

Unit 6: Poetry: 'Colonel Fazackerley'

Overview

English curriculum objectives

- Continue to read and discuss an increasingly wide range of fiction, poetry, plays, non-fiction and reference books or textbooks
- Identify and discuss themes and conventions in and across a wide range of writing
- Learn a wider range of poetry by heart
- Prepare poems and plays to read aloud and to perform, showing understanding through intonation, tone and volume so that the meaning is clear to an audience
- Check that the book makes sense to them, discussing their understanding and exploring the meaning of words in context
- Ask questions to improve their understanding
- Draw inferences such as inferring characters' feelings, thoughts and motives from their actions, and justifying inferences with evidence
- Identify how language, structure and presentation contribute to meaning
- Discuss and evaluate how authors use language, including figurative language, considering the impact on the reader
- Participate in discussions about books that are read to them and those they can read for themselves, building on their own and others' ideas and challenging views courteously
- Explain and discuss their understanding of what they have read, including through formal presentations and debates, maintaining a focus on the topic and using notes where necessary
- Provide reasoned justification for their views

Treasure House resources

- Comprehension Skills Pupil Book 5, Unit 6, pages 19–21
- Collins Connect Treasure House Comprehension Year 5, Unit 6
- Photocopiable Unit 6, Resource 1: Getting the house to yourself, page 95
- Photocopiable Unit 6, Resource 2: Spectre storyboard, page 96

Additional resources

- Dictionaries or the internet
- Other ghostly tales, such as *Three Scary Stories* by Frieda Hughes (optional)

Introduction

Teaching overview

'Colonel Fazackerley' is a comical poem written by Charles Causley. It tells the amusing story of a colonel who buys a castle that, he learns, is haunted by a ghost. The ghost tries its best to frighten the colonel but he is completely unfazed. This sentiment frustrates the ghost into leaving the castle – which, of course, was the Colonel's exact intention.

Introduce the poem

Ask the children if any of them have read any ghost stories, and invite them to share their experiences, and knowledge of ghost stories' characteristics, with the class. Ask if any of them have ever read a ghost story that is funny.

Tell the children that, in this lesson, they will focus on a humorous poem about a haunting. Then they will answer questions about it. Remind children that sometimes the answers to the questions will be clearly written in the poem, but that sometimes they may need to think a little harder and use their own ideas, supported by the text.

Ask the children to read the poem individually or in pairs. Ask them to note down any words they do not understand. Discuss unknown or unusual vocabulary before setting children to work answering the questions in the Pupil Book. Try to avoid discussing the content of the poem until after the children have answered the questions.

Unit 6: Poetry: 'Colonel Fazackerley'

Pupil practice

Pupil Book pages 19–21

Get started

Ask children to write sentences to answer the questions, referring to the text where possible.

Suggested answers

1. Colonel Fazackerley bought an old castle. [1 mark]
2. Colonel Fazackerley was drinking a fine sherry wine on his first evening in his new home. [1 mark]
3. Colonel Fazackerley put down his glass when he first saw the ghost. [1 mark]
4. When he first met the ghost, the colonel called him 'My dear fellow'. [1 mark]
5. When the colonel invited the ghost to sit down and have a drink, the ghost gave a roar. [1 mark]
6. The colonel says he wants the ghost to come to his house-warming party to give his guests 'a turn'. [1 mark]
7. When the Colonel was delighted by the ghost's actions, he called out 'Encore!' [1 mark]
8. After the ghost disappeared, the Colonel smiled and went for dinner. [1 mark]

Try these

Ask children to write sentences to answer the questions, explaining their answers as fully as they can. The children's answers may be subjective but should be in their own words and well justified, using evidence from either the text or the children's own experiences.

Possible answers

1. Answers should state that the poem has nine verses, each made up of two rhyming couplets. [2 marks]
2. Answers should recognise that the ghost is not friendly, but that the colonel is not afraid of it. The ghost attempts in vain to frighten the colonel. [2 marks]
3. Answers should recognise that the colonel's statement suggests he believes the ghost to be someone wearing a costume. They could add that this relates to the suggestion that the ghost is performing a clever party trick. [2 marks]
4. Answers could suggest that the ghost is 'quite out of his wits' as he is running out of ways to try to frighten the colonel, and/or that he is frustrated as the colonel has found him only amusing. [2 marks]
5. Answers should relate that the ghost vanished, his efforts in vain, and was never seen at the castle again. [2 marks]
6. Answers should grasp that the colonel was smiling as he had always intended to drive the ghost away. [2 marks]
7. Assuming responses to the question above were correct, answers should conclude that the colonel had known the ghost was real from the beginning, and that it was not someone attending a fancy dress ball. [2 marks]
8. Answers should grasp that the poet shows pity for the ghost, calling it 'the poor spectre'. [2 marks]

Now try these

The children's answers will be subjective, but should be well justified where appropriate.

Possible answers

1. Answers could refer to the Colonel's apparent calmness, sense of humour and clever plan. [3 marks max]
2. Answers should be from the Colonel's point of view and be consistent with his character and plan, as detailed by the poem. [3 marks max]
3. Answers could refer to the ghost's initial high hopes for the haunting, realisation of the Colonel's attitude, growing desperation and eventual decision to leave the castle. [3 marks max]
4. The uncertain (ambiguous) ending of the poem allows readers to form their own conclusions and to grasp the colonel's plan for themselves, adding to the poem's humour and creating a better punchline. [1 mark]
5. Open-ended question: Look for relevance to the situation and the perspective of the ghost's character, and the same verse form as the poem. [3 marks max]

Unit 6: Poetry: 'Colonel Fazackerley'

Support, embed & challenge

Support
Support children in understanding the basic plot points of the narrative by assisting groups to rewrite the poem as a very short prose story.

Embed
Use Unit 6 Resource 1: Getting the house to yourself to encourage children to think further about the theme of getting rid of an unwanted guest. Ask children to use the grid to plan their own stories or narrative poems about someone who needs to get rid of someone else.

Challenge
Use Unit 6 Resource 2: Spectre storyboard to challenge children to consider the visual aspects of the story. Ask children to imagine they are directing a television adaptation of the poem, and that they have to plan how each shot will look. Ask: 'What camera positions will there be? What things will you show and when? What dialogue will you include?'

Homework / Additional activities

Castle for sale
Ask the children to design the sales advert that the Colonel looked at before buying the castle, including some subtle hints that the ghost exists!

Collins Connect: Unit 6
Ask the children to complete Unit 6 (see Teach → Year 5 → Comprehension → Unit 6).

Unit 7: Non-fiction (formal letter): 'Noisy neighbour'

Overview

English curriculum objectives

- Continue to read and discuss an increasingly wide range of fiction, poetry, plays, non-fiction and reference books or textbooks
- Read books that are structured in different ways and read for a range of purposes
- Identify and discuss themes and conventions in and across a wide range of writing
- Check that the book makes sense to them, discussing their understanding and exploring the meaning of words in context
- Ask questions to improve their understanding
- Summarise the main ideas drawn from more than one paragraph, identifying key details that support the main idea
- Identify how language, structure and presentation contribute to meaning
- Distinguish between statements of fact and opinion
- Retrieve, record and present information from non-fiction
- Participate in discussions about books that are read to them and those they can read for themselves, building on their own and others' ideas and challenging views courteously
- Explain and discuss their understanding of what they have read, including through formal presentations and debates, maintaining a focus on the topic and using notes where necessary
- Provide reasoned justification for their views

Treasure House resources

- Comprehension Skills Pupil Book 5, Unit 7, pages 22–24
- Collins Connect Treasure House Comprehension Year 5, Unit 7
- Photocopiable Unit 7, Resource 1: Three diaries, page 97
- Photocopiable Unit 7, Resource 2: A letter of complaint, page 98

Additional resources

- Dictionaries or the internet

Introduction

Teaching overview

'Noisy neighbour' is a letter from a local council complaints officer, Mr B. Quiet, to a resident who has been persistently noisy. Written in a formal style, the letter warns there will be consequences should the man in question not reduce his noise levels. The text provides an opportunity to explore the characteristics of formal letters and their purpose.

Introduce the text

Ask the children if any of them can suggest reasons why someone might need to write a formal complaint letter. Take suggestions and make notes on the board. Then ask them what they think the features of a formal complaint letter might be.

Tell the children that, in this lesson, they will focus on a formal letter to a man who makes too much noise for his neighbours. Then they will answer questions about it. Remind children that sometimes the answers to the questions will be clearly written in the text, but that sometimes they may need to think a little harder and use their own ideas, supported by the text.

Ask the children to read the letter individually or in pairs. Ask them to note down any words they do not understand. Discuss unknown or unusual vocabulary before setting children to work answering the questions in the Pupil Book. Try to avoid discussing the content of the text until after the children have answered the questions.

Unit 7: Non-fiction (formal letter): 'Noisy neighbour'

Pupil practice

Pupil Book pages 22–24

Get started

Ask children to write sentences to answer the questions, referring to the text where possible.

Suggested answers

1. Mr B. Quiet wrote the letter, from the Environmental Health Department, Southborough Council, High Street, Southborough. [1 mark]
2. Mr J. Trigger is meant to receive the letter. He lives at 9 Hornsey Lane, Southborough. [1 mark]
3. The purpose of the letter is to urge Mr Trigger to stop disturbing his neighbours with unreasonable noise levels. [2 marks]
4. The complaints were made by Mr Trigger's neighbour(s). [1 mark]
5. The examples of offensive behaviour mentioned are: the volume of the music being played from early morning until midnight; the sound of dogs constantly fighting; musical instruments being played at loud volumes; and household appliances being used incessantly. [4 marks max]
6. No, Mr Trigger does not live alone: Mr Quiet refers to other members of his family. [1 mark]
7. Mr Quiet first wrote to Mr Trigger on 29 July. [1 mark]
8. Mr Quiet has written to Mr Trigger three times in total. Mr Trigger has replied twice. [1 mark]

Try these

Ask children to write sentences to answer the questions, explaining their answers as fully as they can. The children's answers may be subjective but should be in their own words and well justified, using evidence from either the text or the children's own experiences.

Possible answers

1. Answers should recognise that Mr Trigger's neighbour wanted the noise to stop. [2 marks]
2. Answers could suggest that Mr Trigger's neighbour may have tried to complain in person but got nowhere and so complained to the council, that he was nervous of approaching Mr Trigger and so complained to the council, or that he simply wanted to make his complaints official. [2 marks]
3. Answers could suggest that Mr Trigger has tried but failed to reduce his noise, that he does not care about the complaints or, possibly, that he himself is not responsible for the noise. [2 marks]
4. Answers could suggest that 'further action' may mean Mr Trigger being fined or being taken to court. [2 marks]
5. Answers should note that previous letters have not been effective, but could add that this letter also contains a 'final warning'. [2 marks]
6. Answers should consider the perspective of someone troubled by a noisy neighbour for over two months. [2 marks]
7. Answers should consider the perspective and feelings of an official whose letters are ignored, and could note that Mr Quiet's phrasing (such as 'I fear that we have received yet another complaint' and 'your total disregard') suggests he is irritated by the situation. [2 marks]
8. Answers should consider the perspective and feelings of a man who has received several letters about the noise coming from his house, but who has not done anything about it. [2 marks]

Now try these

The children's answers will be subjective, but should be well justified where appropriate.

Possible answers

1. Answers could refer to Mr Trigger's noisy lifestyle, lack of control over his dogs and that fact that he 'disregards' official complaints made about him. [3 marks max]
2. The three features listed could include the addresses and the date, the terms 'Dear Sir' and 'Yours faithfully', the formal wording and the use of the second person. [3 marks max]
3. The new words and phrases suggested should be informal. For example: 'emanating': coming; 'occasion': time; 'forthwith': straight away; 'fulfilled': kept; 'incessantly': all the time; 'restrain': hold back; 'disregard': lack of concern. [7 marks]
4. Answers should recognise that informal language would create the impression of a reduction in professionalism, and reduce both the likelihood that the letter will be taken seriously and the power of the council's threat. [3 marks max]
5. Open-ended question: Look for relevance to the situation and characters established, and for appropriate letter form. Formal language may be used, depending on the children's understanding of Mr Trigger's character. [3 marks max]

Unit 7: Non-fiction (formal letter): 'Noisy neighbour'

Support, embed & challenge

Support
Use Unit 7 Resource 1: Three diaries to support children in thinking about the different viewpoints of the people involved. Children should write a paragraph for each of three diaries: Mr B. Quiet, the complaining neighbour and Mr J. Trigger, describing their opinions and feelings about the situation.

Embed
Use Unit 7 Resource 2: A letter of complaint to encourage children to explore the structure and form of a formal letter of complaint. Ask them to imagine that someone keeps dumping litter all over the school field, meaning they can't play on it, and to write a letter to the council to request their support. Encourage them to use the bullet points on the resource sheet, as well as the extract, as guides for the letter.

Challenge
Challenge the children to imagine what may happen next, and to write a further letter to narrate their ideas. Groups could workshop their ideas first.

Homework / Additional activities

Quiet for the council
Ask the children to research and find examples of their local council's rules regarding noise levels. Afterwards, ask groups to discuss how they might try to control noisy neighbours if the council asked for their help.

Collins Connect: Unit 7
Ask the children to complete Unit 7 (see Teach → Year 5 → Comprehension → Unit 7).

Review unit 1: Fiction (classic): 'Pinocchio' Pupil Book pages 25–26

Get started

Ask children to write sentences to answer the questions, referring to the text where possible.

Suggested answers

1. Gepetto was a woodcutter. [1 mark]
2. Pinocchio got called Wobbly-Head, Wooden-Top and Clumpy-Feet. [1 mark]
3. Pinocchio did not like school at all. [1 mark]
4. Pinocchio decided to run away the first time because he didn't like being called names, and the second time because he didn't like school, didn't make friends, and wanted to see the world and make his fortune. [1 mark]
5. Pinocchio went into the little cottage because it started to rain and he began to feel cold and hungry. [1 mark]
6. Inside the cottage, Pinocchio ate the bread on the table and curled up by the fire. [1 mark]
7. Inside the cottage, Pinocchio met a tiny cricket crawling up the wall. [1 mark]
8. The cricket told Pinocchio that running away is always a foolish idea, that it never makes you happy and that it makes your Mama and Papa very sad. [1 mark]

Try these

Ask children to write sentences to answer the questions, explaining their answers as fully as they can.
The children's answers may be subjective but should be in their own words and well justified, using evidence from either the text or the children's own experiences.

Possible answers

1. Answers should acknowledge that Gepetto created Pinocchio because he and his wife had always wanted their own little boy. [2 marks]
2. Answers could suggest that people in the street called Pinocchio names because he looked different to human people. The names that they call him refer to the way he looks (Wobbly-Head, Wooden-Top and Clumpy-Feet). [2 marks]
3. Answers should conclude that Gepetto and his wife were likely to be very upset about Pinocchio running away. They are certainly relieved when he is returned to them. [2 marks]
4. Answers should infer that Pinocchio enjoyed running away, considered it an adventure and didn't seem to care about how much he was hurting his parents. When he runs away, he describes the way he runs in a positive manner: 'in leaps and bounds, tickety tackety'. [2 marks]
5. Answers could suggest that Pinocchio thought it was acceptable to let himself into the little cottage because the door had been left open and/or because he was in need of shelter. [2 marks]
6. Answers should acknowledge that the cricket thinks Pinocchio's actions are foolish and inconsiderate towards his parents, but could add that, as the cricket is giving Pinocchio this advice, he may believe that Pinocchio is capable of changing. [2 marks]
7. Answers should suggest that the author may repeat the phrase to emphasise that Pinocchio repeatedly runs away, and does so in the same cheerful manner each time. [2 marks]
8. Answers should detect that Pinocchio is narrating his own story. It is told in the first person. [2 marks]

Now try these

The children's answers will be subjective, but should be well justified where appropriate.

Possible answers

1. Answers could refer to Pinocchio's happiness at meeting his Mama and Papa at the beginning of the story, unhappiness when people call him names, enjoyment of running away, disappointment or ambivalence when he is brought back, loneliness and possible boredom at school, optimism when running away again, misery when cold and hungry, relief/pleasure at finding the cottage with food and a fire, and surprise at meeting the cricket. [3 marks max]
2. Answers could refer to Pinocchio's sensitivity, flightiness, loneliness, thoughtlessness, selfishness, optimism, impulsiveness and foolishness. [3 marks max]
3. Answers may infer that the sentence shows Pinocchio to be impulsive and thoughtless because it demonstrates that he doesn't hesitate or consider whose property he is using before he acts. [3 marks max]
4. Open-ended question: Look for relevance to task, consistency of character and theme, imagination and presentation. [3 marks max]
5. Open-ended question: Look for relevance to task, consistency of character and theme, imagination and presentation. [3 marks max]

Unit 8: Fiction (classic): 'The Borrowers'

Overview

English curriculum objectives
- Continue to read and discuss an increasingly wide range of fiction, poetry, plays, non-fiction and reference books or textbooks
- Increase their familiarity with a wide range of books, including myths, legends and traditional stories, modern fiction, fiction from our literary heritage, and books from other cultures and traditions
- Recommend books that they have read to their peers, giving reasons for their choices
- Identify and discuss themes and conventions in and across a wide range of writing
- Make comparisons within and across books
- Check that the book makes sense to them, discussing their understanding and exploring the meaning of words in context
- Ask questions to improve their understanding
- Draw inferences such as inferring characters' feelings, thoughts and motives from their actions, and justifying inferences with evidence
- Predict what might happen from details stated and implied
- Identify how language, structure and presentation contribute to meaning
- Discuss and evaluate how authors use language, including figurative language, considering the impact on the reader
- Participate in discussions about books that are read to them and those they can read for themselves, building on their own and others' ideas and challenging views courteously
- Explain and discuss their understanding of what they have read, including through formal presentations and debates, maintaining a focus on the topic and using notes where necessary
- Provide reasoned justification for their views

Treasure House resources
- Comprehension Skills Pupil Book 5, Unit 8, pages 27–29
- Collins Connect Treasure House Comprehension Year 5, Unit 8
- Photocopiable Unit 8, Resource 1: What the Borrowers took, page 99
- Photocopiable Unit 8, Resource 2: Kate's thoughts, page 100

Additional resources
- Dictionaries or the internet
- *The Borrowers* by Mary Norton, whole text (optional)

Introduction

Teaching overview
The Borrowers is a classic children's novel first published in 1952. It tells the tale of a family of tiny people known as 'Borrowers' because they take things from the humans in the house where they live. It encourages children to draw inferences regarding characters' feelings, thoughts and motives from their actions, and to justify inferences with evidence. There are opportunities to develop children's ability to evaluate how authors use language to portray characters' feelings, thoughts and motives, considering the impact on the reader.

Introduce the extract
Ask the children if any of them know the story *The Borrowers*. If they do, invite them to share their knowledge with the class.

Tell the children that, in this lesson, they will focus on one extract from the story. Then they will answer questions about it. Remind children that sometimes the answers to the questions will be clearly written in the extract, but that sometimes they may need to think a little harder and use their own ideas, supported by the text.

Ask the children to read the extract individually or in pairs. Ask them to note down any words they do not understand. Discuss unknown or unusual vocabulary before setting children to work answering the questions in the Pupil Book. Try to avoid discussing the content of the extract until after the children have answered the questions.

Unit 8: Fiction (classic): 'The Borrowers'

Pupil practice

Pupil Book pages 27–29

Get started

Ask children to write sentences to answer the questions, referring to the text where possible.

Suggested answers

1. Kate and Mrs May are doing 'crochet', a kind of knitting done with a hooked needle. They are making a 'quilt' from crochet, which will be a soft cover for a bed. When Kate continues talking 'hastily' she continues with unnecessary speed. Kate thinks that 'thimbles', which are small covers for fingers while sewing, keep disappearing. When Mrs May 'hesitated' she paused uncertainly. When Mrs May gave a 'startled' glance she looked at Kate in a surprised and alarmed way. [6 marks]
2. Kate had lost her crochet hook. [1 mark]
3. Kate still needed to make 30 more woollen squares. [1 mark]
4. Kate put the crochet hook on the bottom shelf of the book-case by her bed. [1 mark]
5. Kate looked for it on the floor and under the rug. [1 mark]
6. Kate also thinks that safety pins, needles, pencils, match boxes, sealing wax, hair slides, drawing pins, thimbles and blotting paper (**not** hatpins) go missing. (Any three of these items should be listed.) [3 marks]
7. Mrs May thought the Borrowers were responsible for taking the missing items. [1 mark]
8. Mrs May says she has never seen a Borrower. [1 mark]

Try these

Ask children to write sentences to answer the questions, explaining their answers as fully as they can. The children's answers may be subjective but should be in their own words and well justified, using evidence from either the text or the children's own experiences.

Possible answers

1. Answers should recognise that all the lost items are small, and that this suggests the Borrowers are also small. They may also suggest that Borrowers are creative for using such odd items. [1 mark]
2. Answers should note that Mrs May suggests the Borrowers are in 'this house' (so the lost things will be too), but that the items are not 'lying about' because the Borrowers in the house are using them. [1 mark]
3. Answers should recognise that Mrs May laughs suddenly because she realises that what she is saying 'all sounds such nonsense'. [1 mark]
4. Answers could suggest that Mrs May draws a sharp breath because she is surprised or unsettled by Kate's question: she very quickly denies that she has ever seen a Borrower. [1 mark]
5. Answers should refer to Mrs May recalling and probably imagining things that happened 'so very long ago'. [1 mark]
6. Answers could suggest that Kate raised her voice because she was eager and excited for Mrs May to continue, and/or frustrated that Mrs May was avoiding telling the story. [1 mark]
7. Answers could refer to Kate being excited, enthusiastic and/or willing to believe in the Borrowers, and to Mrs May, despite her initial 'smile' and her mentioning the Borrowers 'lightly', making mysterious attempts to avoid talking about them more specifically. [1 mark]
8. Answers should recognise that Kate and Mrs May seem close, but note that the older woman is referred to as 'Mrs May': a relatively formal address. It is unlikely that she is Kate's mother or grandmother. [1 mark]

Now try these

The children's answers will be subjective, but should be well justified where appropriate.

Possible answers

1. Answers should show creative consideration of how Borrowers may repurpose small objects. [3 marks max]
2. Answers could refer to Kate's fondness of crochet, thoughtful nature and requests for evidence of the existence of the Borrowers, and her excitement, enthusiasm and willingness to believe with regards to Mrs May's stories. [3 marks max]
3. The phrases are: 'her own needle flicking steadily in the firelight', 'exclaimed Mrs May lightly', 'in the half light she seemed to smile', 'Mrs May laid down her work', 'she picked up her work again', 'Mrs May laughed suddenly', 'she hesitated', 'Mrs May threw her a startled glance', 'Mrs May drew a sharp breath' and 'She gazed downwards at the upturned face and then she smiled and her eyes slid away into the distance'. [10 marks]
4. Answers could refer to any of the actions given in response to Question 3 above, and could suggest that Mrs May initially refers to the Borrowers happily, becomes worried about talking about them in more depth and eventually starts to remember things that happened a long time ago. [3 marks max]
5. Open-ended question: Look for relevance to the plot and characters established, the perspective and feelings of the Borrowers hearing themselves discussed, and correct punctuation of dialogue. [3 marks max]

Unit 8: Fiction (classic): 'The Borrowers'

Support, embed & challenge

Support
Use Unit 8 Resource 1: What the Borrowers took to support children in understanding the kinds of information given in the passage and the actions of the Borrowers. Ask them to choose six small items the Borrowers may have taken and to illustrate ways these items may be used and what the Borrowers may have made from the items.

Embed
Use Unit 8 Resource 2: Kate's thoughts to encourage children to think more deeply about Kate's responses to the conversation in the extract. Ask them to make notes about what Kate might be thinking at each point of the story.

Challenge
Challenge children to write their own short stories about the Borrowers based on the information in the extract and using their imagination.

Homework / Additional activities

Borrowing objects
Ask children to complete a small craft project by finding a small object at home and building it into a different thing, the right size for a Borrower. For example, a comb could become a stepladder or a matchbox could become a bed.

Collins Connect: Unit 8
Ask the children to complete Unit 8 (see Teach → Year 5 → Comprehension → Unit 8).

Unit 9: Playscript: 'The Lost Gardens'

Overview

English curriculum objectives
- Continue to read and discuss an increasingly wide range of fiction, poetry, plays, non-fiction and reference books or textbooks
- Increase their familiarity with a wide range of books, including myths, legends and traditional stories, modern fiction, fiction from our literary heritage, and books from other cultures and traditions
- Identify and discuss themes and conventions in and across a wide range of writing
- Prepare poems and plays to read aloud and to perform, showing understanding through intonation, tone and volume so that the meaning is clear to an audience
- Check that the book makes sense to them, discussing their understanding and exploring the meaning of words in context
- Ask questions to improve their understanding
- Draw inferences such as inferring characters' feelings, thoughts and motives from their actions, and justifying inferences with evidence
- Identify how language, structure and presentation contribute to meaning
- Discuss and evaluate how authors use language, including figurative language, considering the impact on the reader
- Participate in discussions about books that are read to them and those they can read for themselves, building on their own and others' ideas and challenging views courteously
- Explain and discuss their understanding of what they have read, including through formal presentations and debates, maintaining a focus on the topic and using notes where necessary
- Provide reasoned justification for their views

Treasure House resources
- Comprehension Skills Pupil Book 5, Unit 9, pages 30–32
- Collins Connect Treasure House Comprehension Year 5, Unit 9
- Photocopiable Unit 9, Resource 1: Finding the features, page 101
- Photocopiable Unit 9, Resource 2: Different characters, page 102

Additional resources
- Dictionaries or the internet
- *The Lost Gardens* by Phil Osment, whole text (optional)

Introduction

Teaching overview
The Lost Gardens is a play set in a restored garden at the beginning of the 21st century – and also in the same garden, at the beginning of the 20th century. It tells the story of three children who are transported to World War One and become caught up in the lives of young men sent to fight for their country. In the extract, the children meet a mysterious old woman who already knows their names and who points them in the direction of a 'lost' tropical garden. We also catch a glimpse of the slightly troubled nature of the friendship between the two close friends Jack and Maya, and Emmy, to whom they are (at this point) a little hostile.

Introduce the extract
Ask the children for suggestions about mysterious ways stories could start, and scribe their ideas on the board. Perhaps main characters meet a strange new person, encounter an unusual place or find an object they don't understand.

Tell the children that, in this lesson, they will focus on an extract from the very beginning of a playscript in which mysterious things happen to the main characters. Then they will answer questions about it. Remind children that sometimes the answers to the questions will be clearly written in the extract, but that sometimes they may need to think a little harder and use their own ideas, supported by the text.

Ask the children to read the extract individually or in pairs. Ask them to note down any words they do not understand. Discuss unknown or unusual vocabulary before setting children to work answering the questions in the Pupil Book. Try to avoid discussing the content of the extract until after the children have answered the questions.

Unit 9: Playscript: 'The Lost Gardens'

Pupil practice

Pupil Book pages 30–32

Get started

Ask children to write sentences to answer the questions, referring to the text where possible.

Suggested answers

1. The characters in the play are Jack, Maya, Emmy and the Old Lady. [1 mark]
2. The play is set in a restored garden. [1 mark]
3. In the past, there were plants from all over the world in the gardens. People used to visit the gardens especially to look at them. [1 mark]
4. The children's teacher is called Miss Dickinson. [1 mark]
5. The children are on a school trip to visit the gardens. [1 mark]
6. Jack is holding a map of the gardens. [1 mark]
7. Emmy says that the Old Lady 'looks ancient'. [1 mark]
8. The Old Lady gives Jack a huge rusty key. [1 mark]

Try these

Ask children to write sentences to answer the questions, explaining their answers as fully as they can. The children's answers may be subjective but should be in their own words and well justified, using evidence from either the text or the children's own experiences.

Possible answers

1. Answers should detect that Jack and Maya seem to be close friends, but do not like Emmy. Jack says, 'I think we've lost her'; they try to leave for the tropical garden without her; and Maya says, 'She doesn't really like the same games as us' (although Emmy disagrees). [2 marks]
2. Answers could refer to the fact that Maya thinks Emmy is rude when speaking about the Old Lady, and that Emmy tells Jack and Maya: 'You're in trouble. We're not supposed to go off on our own.' [2 marks]
3. Answers should refer to the Old Lady's attempts to encourage Jack and Maya to include Emmy: she tells them 'you can't leave without Emmy', 'Take her with you' and 'You have to stay together'. [2 marks]
4. Answers could refer to the Old Lady's sympathy for Emmy (she says Emmy is 'having a difficult time at the moment') or speculate that the Old Lady knows more about the children than she appears to. [2 marks]
5. Answers should acknowledge that Maya believes Emmy was rude to the old lady (because Emmy talks about the Old Lady rather than talking to her, and calls her 'ancient'), but that the Old Lady doesn't think Emmy was rude. [2 marks]
6. Open-ended question: Answers will be speculative, but could refer to Emmy's apparent difficulty making friends. [2 marks]
7. Open-ended question: Answers will speculate about the mysterious Old Lady's secret. [2 marks]
8. Open-ended question: Answers will speculate about the mysterious nature of the tropical garden. [2 marks]

Now try these

The children's answers will be subjective, but should be well justified where appropriate.

Possible answers

1. Answers should refer to Maya's puzzlement at being known to the Old Lady and acknowledge that this is the first sign of a mystery or of the supernatural. [3 marks max]
2. Open-ended question: Look for six relevant questions directed at the Old Lady that are not answered by the extract, for example: 'How do you know the children's names? Why has the tropical garden not been discovered? Who are you?' [3 marks max]
3. Diary entries should be from Emmy's point of view and refer to Emmy's lack of friendship with Jack and Maya, her attitude (see answer to 'Try these' Question 2) and the fact that she is apparently 'having a difficult time at the moment'. [3 marks max]
4. Open-ended question: Look for relevance to task, propriety of content to the setting and characters, imagination and presentation. [3 marks max]
5. Open-ended question: Look for passages that contain all of the information from the extract as a narrative that doesn't retain any features of a playscript. [3 marks max]

Support, embed & challenge

Support
Use Unit 9 Resource 1: Finding the features to support children in familiarising themselves with the features of a playscript. Children should label the features with the terms supplied. They could also use coloured pens and highlighters to help with the identifications.

Embed
Use Unit 9 Resource 2: Different characters to encourage children to recognise and consider each of the characters in the extract, using the text to give evidence for their opinions on each character.

Challenge
Challenge children to write the next scene of the playscript, in which the three children enter the tropical garden. As well as thinking about the mystery, ask them to think carefully about the children's relationship with each other and how this might change. Remind them to include the features of playscripts, such as stage directions and who says what.

Homework / Additional activities

Back in time
Reveal events from later in the play (as detailed in the 'Teaching overview' above) and provide the whole text of *The Lost Gardens* if possible. Ask children to research and make notes about what life was like for children during World War One. Ask them to be prepared to share their findings with the class, and to discuss what Maya, Jack and Emmy might encounter when they go back in time.

Collins Connect: Unit 9
Ask the children to complete Unit 9 (see Teach → Year 5 → Comprehension → Unit 9).

Unit 10: Poetry: 'A Smuggler's Song'

Overview

English curriculum objectives

- Continue to read and discuss an increasingly wide range of fiction, poetry, plays, non-fiction and reference books or textbooks
- Identify and discuss themes and conventions in and across a wide range of writing
- Learn a wider range of poetry by heart
- Prepare poems and plays to read aloud and to perform, showing understanding through intonation, tone and volume so that the meaning is clear to an audience
- Check that the book makes sense to them, discussing their understanding and exploring the meaning of words in context
- Ask questions to improve their understanding
- Draw inferences such as inferring characters' feelings, thoughts and motives from their actions, and justifying inferences with evidence
- Identify how language, structure and presentation contribute to meaning
- Discuss and evaluate how authors use language, including figurative language, considering the impact on the reader
- Participate in discussions about books that are read to them and those they can read for themselves, building on their own and others' ideas and challenging views courteously
- Explain and discuss their understanding of what they have read, including through formal presentations and debates, maintaining a focus on the topic and using notes where necessary
- Provide reasoned justification for their views

Treasure House resources

- Comprehension Skills Pupil Book 5, Unit 10, pages 33–35
- Collins Connect Treasure House Comprehension Year 5, Unit 10
- Photocopiable Unit 10, Resource 1: Smugglers, page 103
- Photocopiable Unit 10, Resource 2: Good or bad? page 104

Additional resources

- Dictionaries or the internet
- Other examples of narrative poems (optional)

Introduction

Teaching overview

'A Smuggler's Song' is a poem by Rudyard Kipling published in 1906. It reflects on people's decision to turn a blind eye when smugglers enter their town, and the small luxuries these 'gentlemen' supply. Features such as repetition and rhyming couplets make this poem an enjoyable one for children to recite and analyse.

Introduce the poem

Ask the children if any of them know what a smuggler is – in historical and modern terms. Encourage children to discuss ideas and write some of these on the board. (You may wish to use Unit 10, Resource 1: Smugglers to support children with understanding this term.)

Tell the children that, in this lesson, they will focus on a narrative poem about smugglers. Then they will answer questions about it. Remind children that sometimes the answers to the questions will be clearly written in the poem, but that sometimes they may need to think a little harder and use their own ideas, supported by the text.

Ask the children to read the poem individually or in pairs. Ask them to note down any words they do not understand. Discuss unknown or unusual vocabulary before setting children to work answering the questions in the Pupil Book. Try to avoid discussing the content of the poem until after the children have answered the questions.

Unit 10: Poetry: 'A Smuggler's Song'

Pupil practice

Pupil Book pages 33–35

Get started

Ask children to write sentences to answer the questions, referring to the text where possible.

Suggested answers

1. Many of these terms are difficult and are unlikely to be found in children's dictionaries. A class discussion may be more beneficial than children trying to decipher them alone. A 'smuggler' is a person who illegally sneaks goods, such as brandy and laces, from one place to another. When the smugglers bring 'baccy' they are bringing tobacco. If the children are running around a 'woodlump' they may be running around a tree stump or a pile of firewood. If the barrels are tarred they are covered in 'tar', a sticky black liquid made from coal used to make the barrels waterproof. If the barrels are covered in 'brushwood' they are covered in broken branches and twigs. If the child is 'mindful' about something that is said she thinks carefully about it. If the soldier 'chucks' the child under her chin he taps her lightly and affectionately under her chin. A cap of 'Valenciennes' is a cap of a special kind of lace made in France. [8 marks]

2. The poem's listener should not look out of the window at midnight. [1 mark]

3. The smugglers are bringing brandy for the Parson. [1 mark]

4. The smugglers are bringing the laces for 'the lady'. [1 mark]

5. Through the open stable door the listener might see a tired horse lying down. [1 mark]

6. King George's men are dressed in red and blue. [1 mark]

7. 'Trusty' and 'Pincher' are the house-dogs. [1 mark]

8. If the listener does as she's been told she might be given a dainty doll. [1 mark]

Try these

Ask children to write sentences to answer the questions, explaining their answers as fully as they can. The children's answers may be subjective but should be in their own words and well justified, using evidence from either the text or the children's own experiences.

Possible answers

1. Answers should suggest that the line means something approximating 'mind your own business'. [2 marks]

2. As above, answers should suggest that this line, too, means something approximating 'mind your own business'. [2 marks]

3. Answers should grasp that smuggling is a crime and that King George's men are trying to accost smugglers. [2 marks]

4. Answers could refer to rhyming couplets' potential for lightening the effect of the poem and/or providing an appealing, steady rhythm that sounds like horses' hooves. [2 marks]

5. Answers should start to grasp that the house-dogs are friendly towards the Gentlemen because they know them. [2 marks]

6. Answers should suggest that the speaker is both a smuggler and the father, or another close relative, of the listener. [2 marks]

7. Answers could select almost any of the poem's phrases – all those chosen should hint at the smuggled goods and/or smuggler's belongings being found in or around the listener's home (e.g. 'Running round the woodlump if you chance to find / Little barrels ...'; 'mother mends a coat cut about and tore') or the smuggler's personal relationship with the listener (he calls her 'my darling' and offers her 'a dainty doll'). [2 marks]

8. Answers could refer to the smugglers' illegal occupation or the speaker's kindly manner and provision for respectable people. [2 marks]

Now try these

The children's answers will be subjective, but should be well justified where appropriate.

Possible answers

1. Mind maps could refer to the child's initial worry about or fear of the Gentlemen, her questions about what they do, her realisation that soldiers may be searching for them, and her understanding of what the Gentlemen can bring for her and others. [3 marks max]

2. Answers could refer to the speaker's kind tone, firm warnings, illegal occupation, apparently comfortable home life and/or provision for respectable people. [3 marks max]

3. Open-ended question: Look for relevant details from the extract, imagination, presentation, formal language and consistency with the attitude and purpose of the soldiers: to catch the smugglers. [3 marks max]

4. Answers should refer to the strength of the rhythm (which helps the poem to move along and flow). More specifically, the rhythm gives four stresses per line, although the number of syllables per line varies. Answers should try to relate these features with the content of the poem, for example by suggesting that the contrast, and the flow of the strong rhythm, sounds a little like horses' hooves. [3 marks max]

5. Open-ended question: Look for verses that contain the same detail but that use only modern language. [3 marks max]

Unit 10: Poetry: 'A Smuggler's Song'

Support, embed & challenge

Support
Use Unit 10, Resource 1: Smugglers to provide some background information about smugglers, historically and in modern times. Read through the information with the children and discuss their reactions. Ask them to find facts relevant to the poem.

Embed
Use Unit 10, Resource 2: Good or bad? to encourage children to consider whether smugglers, in the context of the poem, were good or bad. Ask them to reread the poem and to sort its impressions of smugglers into the two columns. You could then ask them to add ideas from wider research to the table, too.

Challenge
Challenge children to write at least three more verses for the poem about what might happen next. Ask: 'What might the child do?' Ask children to think carefully about the rhymes and rhythm they will use in their verses.

Homework / Additional activities

Ask me no questions…
Ask children to compose their own poems about keeping secrets, all with the title 'Ask me no questions and I'll tell you no lies'.

Collins Connect: Unit 10
Ask the children to complete Unit 10 (see Teach → Year 5 → Comprehension → Unit 10).

Unit 11: Poetry: 'From a Railway Carriage'

Overview

English curriculum objectives

- Continue to read and discuss an increasingly wide range of fiction, poetry, plays, non-fiction and reference books or textbooks
- Identify and discuss themes and conventions in and across a wide range of writing
- Learn a wider range of poetry by heart
- Prepare poems and plays to read aloud and to perform, showing understanding through intonation, tone and volume so that the meaning is clear to an audience
- Check that the book makes sense to them, discussing their understanding and exploring the meaning of words in context
- Ask questions to improve their understanding
- Draw inferences such as inferring characters' feelings, thoughts and motives from their actions, and justifying inferences with evidence
- Identify how language, structure and presentation contribute to meaning
- Discuss and evaluate how authors use language, including figurative language, considering the impact on the reader
- Participate in discussions about books that are read to them and those they can read for themselves, building on their own and others' ideas and challenging views courteously
- Explain and discuss their understanding of what they have read, including through formal presentations and debates, maintaining a focus on the topic and using notes where necessary
- Provide reasoned justification for their views

Treasure House resources

- Comprehension Skills Pupil Book 5, Unit 11, pages 36–38
- Collins Connect Treasure House Comprehension Year 5, Unit 11
- Photocopiable Unit 11, Resource 1: Finding the beat, page 105
- Photocopiable Unit 11, Resource 2: A mind map, page 106

Additional resources

- Dictionaries or the internet
- Other poems and/or non-fiction text about railways (optional)

Introduction

Teaching overview

When Robert Louis Stevenson wrote 'From a Railway Carriage' in the 19th century, travel by steam was transforming people's lives. Journeys by train would have been an astonishing experience: both awe-inspiring and, for some, terrifying. Stevenson demonstrates the magic of a train ride through his rattling, train-like rhythm as well as his descriptions of the rapidly passing scenery.

Introduce the poem

Ask the children if they have ever travelled by train – or even by steam train. If they have, ask them to describe what their journey was like. Then ask the children to imagine what it would have been like travelling on a steam train when they were first invented. Explain that this would certainly be the fastest they had ever travelled!

Tell the children that, in this lesson, they will focus on a poem about travelling by steam train. Then they will answer questions about it. Remind children that sometimes the answers to the questions will be clearly written in the poem, but that sometimes they may need to think a little harder and use their own ideas, supported by the text.

Ask the children to read the poem individually or in pairs. Ask them to note down any words they do not understand. Discuss unknown or unusual vocabulary before setting children to work answering the questions in the Pupil Book. Try to avoid discussing the content of the poem until after the children have answered the questions.

Unit 11: Poetry: 'From a Railway Carriage'

Pupil practice

Pupil Book pages 36–38

Get started

Ask children to write sentences to answer the questions, referring to the text where possible.

Suggested answers

1. 'Ditches' are narrow channels dug at the side of roads or fields, to hold or carry away water. If the train is 'charging' it is moving quickly and forcefully. 'Driving' rain is rain being blown by the wind with great force. The child who 'clambers' is climbing or moving in an awkward and laborious way. 'Brambles' are prickly blackberry bushes. A 'glimpse' is a brief and momentary view, such as those from the moving train's window. [6 marks]

2. According to the poem, all the sights of the hill and the plain (the views from the train window) are flying 'as thick as driving rain'. [1 mark]

3. According to the poem, the views of horses and cattle seem to be 'charging along like troops in a battle'. [1 mark]

4. The train stations are described as 'whistling by'. [1 mark]

5. The child clambers, scrambles and gathers brambles. [1 mark]

6. The tramp is standing and gazing at the train. [1 mark]

7. The man and cart are described as 'lumping along'. [1 mark]

8. The word 'and' is used 14 times in the poem. [1 mark]

Try these

Ask children to write sentences to answer the questions, explaining their answers as fully as they can. The children's answers may be subjective but should be in their own words and well justified, using evidence from either the text or the children's own experiences.

Possible answers

1. Answers should recognise that the poem gives the reader the impression that the train is moving along quickly. [2 marks]

2. Answers could suggest that the poet refers to 'fairies' and 'witches' in order to make the train seem magical. [2 marks]

3. Answers could suggest that the tramp is gazing at the train because he may not have seen one before, and/or may never be able to afford to ride on a train. [1 mark]

4. Answers should recognise that the poet describes the bridges, houses, hedges and ditches as moving because, from the perspective of someone looking out from a railway carriage, it seems that they are moving rather than the train. [2 marks]

5. Answers could suggest that the effect of the word 'and' being used so frequently is to create a feeling of on-going movement, just like being on a train journey. [2 marks]

6. Answers should conclude that the poem is meant to be read swiftly, at a rattling pace that mimics the train's movement. [2 marks]

7. Answers should grasp that the phrase 'each a glimpse and gone for ever' refers to how quickly each sight is seen before it is gone, as the train quickly moves on. [2 marks]

8. Answers should recognise that the rail industry boom meant that many people were witnessing train travel for the first time, and that this sense of newness, excitement and mystery influenced the poem. [2 marks]

Now try these

The children's answers will be subjective, but should be well justified where appropriate.

Possible answers

1. Monitor the children's performances. The poem should be read swiftly, and children should recognise that its steady, rattling rhythm sounds similar to a chugging steam train. [3 marks max]

2. Answers should conclude that the poet has created this effect by carefully choosing the amount of words and syllables per line. Specifically, there are four beats per line and, generally, a stressed syllable followed by two or three unstressed syllables. [3 marks max]

3. The similes are 'charging along like troops in a battle' and 'fly as thick as driving rain'. Answers could suggest that these are used to help the reader to draw comparisons and imagine the experience of speed described in the poem. [3 marks max]

4. Open-ended question: The two rhyming couplets should be from the child's point of view. Look for consistency with the poem's style and theme, imagination and presentation. [3 marks max]

5. Open-ended question: Look for relevance to task, consistency of theme, imagination and presentation. [3 marks max]

Unit 11: Poetry: 'From a Railway Carriage'

Support, embed & challenge

Support
Use Unit 11 Resource 1: Finding the beat to support children in familiarising themselves with the rhythm of the extract. Children should count and mark each line's syllables and beats, following the example. They could also use coloured pens and highlighters to identify instances of repetition and description.

Embed
Use Unit 11 Resource 2: A mind map to encourage children to explore the way a modern train moves, and how it feels to travel on one, in order to help them compose their own poems. Ask the children to complete the mind map, thinking carefully about their descriptions of what they may (or may not) see through the window. Ask: 'Might the sights seem to be moving, instead of the train?' When the children begin to write their poems, ask them to think carefully about the rhythm they will use.

Challenge
Challenge children to discuss similes further. Ask them to remind themselves of the similes in the poem and then to come up with as many similes as they can to describe railway travel.

Homework / Additional activities

A travel journal
Ask the children to write diary extracts as if they are passengers on the train in 'From a Railway Carriage'. Remind them that this journey would almost certainly be their first experience of train travel.

Collins Connect: Unit 11
Ask the children to complete Unit 11 (see Teach → Year 5 → Comprehension → Unit 11).

Unit 12: Non-fiction (instructions): 'Magic matchsticks'

Overview

English curriculum objectives

- Continue to read and discuss an increasingly wide range of fiction, poetry, plays, non-fiction and reference books or textbooks
- Read books that are structured in different ways and read for a range of purposes
- Identify and discuss themes and conventions in and across a wide range of writing
- Check that the book makes sense to them, discussing their understanding and exploring the meaning of words in context
- Ask questions to improve their understanding
- Summarise the main ideas drawn from more than one paragraph, identifying key details that support the main idea
- Identify how language, structure and presentation contribute to meaning
- Distinguish between statements of fact and opinion
- Retrieve, record and present information from non-fiction
- Participate in discussions about books that are read to them and those they can read for themselves, building on their own and others' ideas and challenging views courteously
- Explain and discuss their understanding of what they have read, including through formal presentations and debates, maintaining a focus on the topic and using notes where necessary
- Provide reasoned justification for their views

Treasure House resources

- Comprehension Skills Pupil Book 5, Unit 12, pages 39–41
- Collins Connect Treasure House Comprehension Year 5, Unit 12
- Photocopiable Unit 12, Resource 1: Making a cup of tea, page 107
- Photocopiable Unit 12, Resource 2: Writing a recipe, page 108

Additional resources

- Dictionaries or the internet
- Other examples of instructions (optional)
- Several matchsticks and a handkerchief with hems along the edges (optional)

Introduction

Teaching overview

'Magic Matchsticks' gives step-by-step instructions for performing a magic trick using matchsticks and a handkerchief. The text displays characteristics common to instructional writing: an introductory paragraph, a resource list, numbered instructions, and clear and concise explanations that use imperative verbs and clearly labelled diagrams. If you have the resources, you may wish to invite children to try performing the trick after they have read the text.

Introduce the text

Ask the children to describe the purpose of instructions, and scribe their responses on the board. Then ask them to give examples of instructions they encounter in everyday life (such as recipes or instructions for new games). Again, note down their suggestions.

Tell the children that, in this lesson, they will focus on a set of instructions for a magic trick. Then they will answer questions about it. Remind children that sometimes the answers to the questions will be clearly written in the text, but that sometimes they may need to think a little harder and use their own ideas, supported by the text.

Ask the children to read the text individually or in pairs. Ask them to note down any words they do not understand. Discuss unknown or unusual vocabulary before setting children to work answering the questions in the Pupil Book. Try to avoid discussing the content of the text until after the children have answered the questions.

Unit 12: Non-fiction (instructions): 'Magic matchsticks'

Pupil practice

Pupil Book pages 39–41

Get started
Ask children to write sentences to answer the questions, referring to the text where possible.

Suggested answers

1. Put a <u>short, thin stick</u> into the <u>folded-over and sewn-down edge</u> of a <u>square piece of material you might use to wipe your nose</u>. <u>Practise</u> the trick <u>properly and carefully</u>. Your friends will be <u>amazed</u>, if they don't become <u>questioning and doubtful</u> of you! [7 marks]
2. The instructions will help the reader to perform a magic trick. [1 mark]
3. You need several matches and a handkerchief with a hem to perform the trick. [1 mark]
4. A magician's real secret is in rehearsing thoroughly before showing anyone his or her tricks. [1 mark]
5. Before you try the trick on your family, you should practise it thoroughly. [1 mark]
6. Step 1 is to show the audience a matchstick. [1 mark]
7. The secret of the trick is that there are two matches: one already hidden inside the hem of the handkerchief. [1 mark]
8. Before you perform the trick, you need to prepare by setting up several handkerchiefs with matchsticks inside their hems. [1 mark]

Try these
Ask children to write sentences to answer the questions, explaining their answers as fully as they can. The children's answers may be subjective but should be in their own words and well justified, using evidence from either the text or the children's own experiences.

Possible answers

1. Answers should refer to the importance of appearing to prove to the audience that there is nothing hidden in the handkerchief. [2 marks]
2. Answers should refer to tricks needing to look perfect, and the idea that practice reduces the likelihood of mistakes. [2 marks]
3. Answers could suggest that the second matchstick could fall out, that the wrong matchstick could get snapped or that the audience may notice you swapping handkerchiefs and become suspicious. [2 marks]
4. Answers should refer to the possibility that the audience will ask to see the trick again. [2 marks]
5. Answers should refer to the effectiveness of the trick and that fact that audience members may be impressed. [2 marks]
6. Answers should refer to the possibility that the audience will guess that the handkerchiefs had to be prepared earlier. [2 marks]
7. Answers could refer to the instructions' clear sections and numbering, and/or to the fact that they explain 'the secret' at the end, rather than in the correct (chronological) place in the instructions. [2 marks]
8. Answers could refer to moving 'the secret' to earlier in the instructions, or any further sensible improvements. [2 marks]

Now try these
The children's answers will be subjective, but should be well justified where appropriate.

Possible answers

1. Answers should be from the audience's point of view and as though ignorant of 'the secret' of the trick. [3 marks max]
2. Answers should refer to the introduction, different sections, list of things you need, numbered instructions, description of 'the secret' and the diagram. [3 marks max]
3. The new numbered list should begin with the set-up and include ensuring that the audience member snaps the match in the handkerchief's hem. [3 marks max]
4. Open-ended question: Look for relevance to task and clear numbered instructions. [3 marks max]
5. Open-ended question: Look for relevance to task and references to an introduction, different sections, list of things you need, numbered instructions and/or a diagram. [3 marks max]

Support, embed & challenge

Support
Use Unit 12 Resource 1: Making a cup of tea to support children in checking their knowledge and understanding about instructions. Ask children to cut out the instructions and put them in a sensible order, and then to add numbers, diagrams to help the reader and a title.

Embed
Use Unit 12 Resource 2: Writing a recipe to encourage children to write their own set of instructions. Ask children to write instructions for a simple recipe (such as for making cheese on toast).

Challenge
Challenge children to research instructions for other magic tricks. Ask partners to test the effectiveness of the instructions they find by trying out the tricks.

Unit 12: Non-fiction (instructions): 'Magic matchsticks'

Homework / Additional activities

The importance of instructions
Ask children to find out more about how useful instructions can be. Ask them to interview adult friends or family members to find out what kinds of instructions they use and how they use them.

Collins Connect: Unit 12
Ask the children to complete Unit 12 (see Teach → Year 5 → Comprehension → Unit 12).

Unit 13: Non-fiction (historical): 'The Trojan War'

Overview

English curriculum objectives

- Continue to read and discuss an increasingly wide range of fiction, poetry, plays, non-fiction and reference books or textbooks
- Read books that are structured in different ways and read for a range of purposes
- Identify and discuss themes and conventions in and across a wide range of writing
- Check that the book makes sense to them, discussing their understanding and exploring the meaning of words in context
- Ask questions to improve their understanding
- Summarise the main ideas drawn from more than one paragraph, identifying key details that support the main idea
- Draw inferences such as inferring characters' feelings, thoughts and motives from their actions, and justifying inferences with evidence
- Predict what might happen from details stated and implied
- Identify how language, structure and presentation contribute to meaning
- Distinguish between statements of fact and opinion
- Retrieve, record and present information from non-fiction
- Participate in discussions about books that are read to them and those they can read for themselves, building on their own and others' ideas and challenging views courteously
- Explain and discuss their understanding of what they have read, including through formal presentations and debates, maintaining a focus on the topic and using notes where necessary
- Provide reasoned justification for their views

Treasure House resources

- Comprehension Skills Pupil Book 5, Unit 13, pages 42–44
- Collins Connect Treasure House Comprehension Year 5, Unit 13
- Photocopiable Unit 13, Resource 1: Quick quiz, page 109
- Photocopiable Unit 13, Resource 2: A Trojan comic strip, page 110

Additional resources

- Dictionaries or the internet
- Other non-fiction texts about life in ancient Greece (optional)

Introduction

Teaching overview

'The Trojan War' is a non-fiction historical recount text about the epic war between the ancient Greek and Trojan armies. The Trojan War is considered to be one of the most important events in ancient history, but many historians still debate how true the accounts of it are. 'The Trojan War' is an interesting text for children to explore, given its part-truth, part-legend roots.

Introduce the text

Ask the children if any of them know anything about ancient Greek life or stories. If they do, invite them to share their knowledge with the class.

Tell the children that, in this lesson, they will focus on a non-fiction historical text about the Trojan War. Then they will answer questions about it. Remind children that sometimes the answers to the questions will be clearly written in the text, but that sometimes they may need to think a little harder and use their own ideas, supported by the text.

Ask the children to read the text individually or in pairs. Ask them to note down any words they do not understand. Discuss unknown or unusual vocabulary before setting children to work answering the questions in the Pupil Book. Try to avoid discussing the content of the text until after the children have answered the questions.

Unit 13: Non-fiction (historical): 'The Trojan War'

Pupil practice

Pupil Book pages 42–44

Get started

Ask children to write sentences to answer the questions, referring to the text where possible.

Suggested answers

1. Troy was one of the greatest cities in the ancient world. [1 mark]
2. Troy was considered impenetrable because it was surrounded by huge, mighty walls. [1 mark]
3. Paris was one of the Trojan princes who lived in the city. [1 mark]
4. The most beautiful woman Paris had ever seen was Helen, who was the wife of King Menelaus. [1 mark]
5. When King Menelaus found out that Helen was gone, the first thing he did was to send his messengers to ask the Trojans to return her. [1 mark]
6. Achilles was a Greek hero who fought in the Trojan War. He was special because he was the son of Zeus and because he was almost completely protected from harm by the magic waters of the Styx River. [1 mark]
7. Achilles was killed when Paris shot him in his heel with a poisoned arrow. [1 mark]
8. Odysseus came up with the idea for the Trojan horse. [1 mark]

Try these

Ask children to write sentences to answer the questions, explaining their answers as fully as they can. The children's answers may be subjective but should be in their own words and well justified, using evidence from either the text or the children's own experiences.

Possible answers

1. Answers should refer to formal, historical language. They could refer to it setting the tone for a trustworthy historical recount or tale from the ancient world. [2 marks]
2. Answers should acknowledge that historical recounts are usually factual, but could express doubt that the Trojans would be taken in by the plan, or refer to less believable sections of the recount (see below). [2 marks]
3. Answers could be sceptical of the concepts of half-gods and/or magical waters. [2 marks]
4. Answers could refer to Sinon's loyalty to the Greeks and his intentions to sneak them into Troy. [2 marks]
5. Answers should refer to the Trojans being 'intrigued' and could also infer their suspicion of the horse from their behaviour towards it and Sinon. [2 marks]
6. Answers could consider Helen's love for Paris, fear of Menelaus's anger, regret of her actions and/or possible relief at returning to Greece. [1 mark]
7. Answers could suggest that the Greeks' trick was either clever or treacherous. [2 marks]
8. Answers could consider Paris's charm, Menelaus's/Agamemnon's leadership of the Greeks, Achilles' power and strength, Odysseus's clever plan or Sinon's bravery. [2 marks]

Now try these

The children's answers will be subjective, but should be well justified where appropriate.

Possible answers

1. All words suggested should be modern and show understanding of the original terms. For example: 'impenetrable': unbreakable; 'eloped': ran away; 'bewilderment': confusion; 'thus': in this way; 'hitherto' until now; 'invincible': undefeated; 'devised': came up with; 'unbeknown': unknown; 'flocked': crowded; 'intrigued': interested/fascinated; 'divulge': let slip; 'demoralised': upset; 'rout': huge defeat. [13 marks]
2. Answers could refer to Paris's charm, powers of persuasion, lack of feeling for Menelaus, foolishness for causing a war, romantic nature and/or cleverness in defeating Achilles. [3 marks max]
3. Answers could refer to Menelaus's initial eagerness to meet Paris, his 'bewilderment and anger' at Helen's departure, his hopes to get her back, his planning when assembling his army, his sadness at losing Achilles, his pleasure with Odysseus's plan, his victory when Greece won the war and/or his relief/resentment when Helen returned. [3 marks max]
4. Open-ended question: Answers should refer to the facts from the extract but be in the children's own words. [3 marks max]
5. Open-ended question: Look for relevance to task, consistency of characters and theme, imagination, presentation and correct punctuation for dialogue. [3 marks max]

Unit 13: Non-fiction (historical): 'The Trojan War'

Support, embed & challenge

Support
Use Unit 13 Resource 1: Quick quiz to support children in grounding the knowledge they have gained from the extract as they create a short quiz on it. Ask children to come up with five questions that the extract can answer, and then swap their quiz with a partner.

Embed
Use Unit 13 Resource 2: A Trojan comic strip to encourage children to explore the events in the extract. Ask children to retell a part of the story using a comic strip layout and style. Support them in thinking about how they will divide the section into the number of boxes given in the comic strip template, and how they will use the thought and speech bubbles. Support children in summarising each scene to retell the story using minimal words.

Challenge
Challenge children to consider how the events described in the extract might be presented differently if they were retold using informal, modern language. Ask the children to write a draft of an email to a friend, retelling part or all of the events in the text using modern language.

Homework / Additional activities

More about Troy
Ask children to research more about the Trojan War using library books or the internet. Ask them to consider what things they consider likely to be factual, and to be prepared to share their findings with the class or a group.

Collins Connect: Unit 13
Ask the children to complete Unit 13 (see Teach → Year 5 → Comprehension → Unit 13).

Unit 14: Fiction (legend): 'Shen Nung'

Overview

English curriculum objectives

- Continue to read and discuss an increasingly wide range of fiction, poetry, plays, non-fiction and reference books or textbooks
- Increase their familiarity with a wide range of books, including myths, legends and traditional stories, modern fiction, fiction from our literary heritage, and books from other cultures and traditions
- Recommend books that they have read to their peers, giving reasons for their choices
- Identify and discuss themes and conventions in and across a wide range of writing
- Make comparisons within and across books
- Check that the book makes sense to them, discussing their understanding and exploring the meaning of words in context
- Ask questions to improve their understanding
- Draw inferences such as inferring characters' feelings, thoughts and motives from their actions, and justifying inferences with evidence
- Predict what might happen from details stated and implied
- Identify how language, structure and presentation contribute to meaning
- Discuss and evaluate how authors use language, including figurative language, considering the impact on the reader
- Participate in discussions about books that are read to them and those they can read for themselves, building on their own and others' ideas and challenging views courteously
- Explain and discuss their understanding of what they have read, including through formal presentations and debates, maintaining a focus on the topic and using notes where necessary
- Provide reasoned justification for their views

Treasure House resources

- Comprehension Skills Pupil Book 5, Unit 14, pages 45–47
- Collins Connect Treasure House Comprehension Year 5, Unit 14
- Photocopiable Unit 14, Resource 1: Shen Nung's character, page 111
- Photocopiable Unit 14, Resource 2: An important discovery, page 112

Additional resources

- Dictionaries or the internet
- Other myths and legends (optional)

Introduction

Teaching overview

'Shen Nung' is a legend based on a Chinese emperor who was deified and is remembered as the god of medicine. According to legend, he invented the plough, discovered tea and ginseng, and taught his people how to farm effectively and use plants in medicine. Like Unit 13, this is an interesting text for children to explore, given its part-truth, part-legend roots.

Introduce the legend

Ask the children if they have heard of or know anything about Chinese legends. If they do, invite them to share their knowledge with the class. Then ask what the children know about the form and conventions of legends in general, and briefly discuss this.

Tell the children that, in this lesson, they will focus on a legend about a Chinese emperor called Shen Nung. Then they will answer questions about it. Remind children that sometimes the answers to the questions will be clearly written in the story, but that sometimes they may need to think a little harder and use their own ideas, supported by the text.

Ask the children to read the story individually or in pairs. Ask them to note down any words they do not understand. Discuss unknown or unusual vocabulary before setting children to work answering the questions in the Pupil Book. Try to avoid discussing the content of the story until after the children have answered the questions.

Pupil practice

Pupil Book pages 45–47

Get started

Ask children to write sentences to answer the questions, referring to the text where possible.

Suggested answers

1. The great 'civilisation' of China refers to its society or culture at a particular time in history. Farmers used a 'plough' to turn over the soil in the fields. The plough would be pulled by an 'ox', which was a bull. The farmers wanted to 'cultivate' their crops, meaning they wanted to grow and develop them. When Shen Nung 'strained' the tea he put it through a sieve. Ginseng removed any 'impurities', or any unclean parts, from the blood. China is 'renowned', or famous, for silk cloth. Shen Nung and his wife were 'deified', which means they were made into gods. Western countries were still 'primitive': they were still at an early stage of development and civilisation. [9 marks]

2. China's age of the 'Great Ten' was when each of 10 successive emperors brought new skills and knowledge to it. [1 mark]

3. Some legends described Shen Nung's head as 'the head of an ox'. [1 mark]

4. Shen Nung taught his people to create productive land by felling trees and burning the stumps to create space and enrich the soil. [1 mark]

5. Shen Nung was remembered as the god of medicine. [1 mark]

6. According to the extract, ginseng is a plant whose roots clean the blood of impurities. It can make tired people feel energetic and older people feel younger. [1 mark]

7. According to the legend, Shen Nung died when a strange, sharp form of grass cut his stomach to ribbons. [1 mark]

8. Shen Nung's wife is remembered for mastering the art of breeding silkworms to create silk, and as the goddess of housecrafts. [1 mark]

Try these

Ask children to write sentences to answer the questions, explaining their answers as fully as they can. The children's answers may be subjective but should be in their own words and well justified, using evidence from either the text or the children's own experiences.

Possible answers

1. Answers should refer to the importance of medicine, tea, farming and fine cloth to the success of China as a country. [2 marks]

2. Answers should refer to the effects of medicine, tea, effective farming and fine cloth on people's lives. [2 marks]

3. Answers should refer to the necessity of growing crops well to create more food for people and more income for farmers. [2 marks]

4. Answers should conclude that much of the information in the extract will have been based on fact. [2 marks]

5. Answers could suggest that the untrue elements explain things people didn't understand, or that the legends' writer(s) wanted to add magical or mysterious elements to stories. [2 marks]

6. Answers could suggest that the untrue information makes the legend more exciting and impressive, or that it reduces the likelihood that the true elements will be believed. [2 marks]

7. Answers should refer to the facts that oxen were said to pull ploughs on farms and that Shen Nung invented the plough. [2 marks]

8. Answers should suggest that being deified was an honour given to people who had contributed a lot to society. [2 marks]

Now try these

The children's answers will be subjective, but should be well justified where appropriate.

Possible answers

1. Mind maps could refer to farming (including the plough), medicine (including ginseng) and tea, and include details about how these things influence life then and now. [3 marks max]

2. Open-ended question: Look for relevance to task, imagination and presentation. [3 marks max]

3. Open-ended question: Look for six relevant questions directed at Shen Nung that are not answered by the extract, for example: 'How did you invent the plough?' 'Do you really have the head of an ox?' 'Which was your favourite discovery?' [3 marks max]

4. Open-ended question: Look for relevance to task, consistency of character and theme, imagination, presentation and correct punctuation for dialogue. [3 marks max]

5. Open-ended question: Diary entries should be written from the point of view of Shen Nung. Look for relevance to the discovery of ginseng, consistency of character and theme, imagination, presentation and reference to the details in the extract, including those that seem to be untrue. [3 marks max]

Unit 14: Fiction (legend): 'Shen Nung'

Support, embed & challenge

Support
Use Unit 14 Resource 1: Shen Nung's character to support children in exploring the character and achievements of Shen Nung further. Children should reread the text carefully to extract information that they can use in the profile.

Embed
Ask children to rewrite the legend of Shen Nung in the first person, from the point of view of Shen Nung himself.

Challenge
Use Unit 14 Resource 2: An important discovery to challenge children to research someone else who discovered or developed something important. It could be an important scientist or a designer. The information could be entirely factual or, like the legend of Shen Nung, children's reports could include some fictional parts.

Homework / Additional activities

Legend hunting
Ask children to find other legends and to think carefully about their content. Ask them to study what things they think are likely to be based on truth and what things they think are likely to be fictional. Ask them to be prepared to share their findings with the class or a group.

Collins Connect: Unit 14
Ask the children to complete Unit 14 (see Teach → Year 5 → Comprehension → Unit 14).

Review unit 2: Non-fiction (information text): 'Your Brain'

Pupil Book pages 48–49

Get started

Ask children to write sentences to answer the questions, referring to the text where possible.

Suggested answers

1. The extract says your brain is the control centre of your body. [1 mark]
2. Your brain works 24 hours a day, seven days a week for the whole of your life. [1 mark]
3. Your brain controls everything that's going on in your body. [1 mark]
4. The extract says that we (humans) can read, write and learn languages – these are things other animals can't do. [1 mark]
5. Your brain is found inside your head. [1 mark]
6. An adult's brain weighs about 1.4 kilograms. [1 mark]
7. Brains look pinky-white on the outside and grey-white on the inside. [1 mark]
8. Your brain is made up of billions of cells. [1 mark]

Try these

Ask children to write sentences to answer the questions, explaining their answers as fully as they can. The children's answers may be subjective but should be in their own words and well justified, using evidence from either the text or the children's own experiences.

Possible answers

1. Answers should recognise that there are no straightforward opinions in the text. (However, the word 'surprisingly' does suggest an opinion about what is surprising.) [2 marks]
2. Answers should recognise that the extract is written in an accessible, personal tone, because it uses personal pronouns such as 'you' and 'our', and that this engages the reader in a friendly way. (This may be more appropriate in a children's text than it would be in an adult's.) [2 marks]
3. Answers should recognise that the photograph of the newborn baby is useful because it provides the reader with an example of the proportions of a baby's head and body (which is the topic being discussed). [2 marks]
4. Open-ended question: The child's choice should be justified. [2 marks]
5. Answers should recognise that readers may find the text interesting or informative if they wish to learn more about their brains and how they work. [2 marks]
6. Answers could conclude that it is important for humans to understand the way our bodies work in order for medical knowledge and other physical understanding to progress, and in order for people to stay healthy. Alternatively, they may assert that that it is not important for humans to understand the way our bodies work on a day-to-day basis, perhaps because they will continue to work whether or not we understand them. [2 marks]
7. Answers should recognise that the author is likely to have conducted thorough research about brains in order to write the book. [2 marks]
8. Open-ended question: Answers could suggest that the text doesn't tell you details about how the brain controls the body, which parts of the brain perform which tasks, whether the brain can recover from being damaged, how surgeons operate on the brain or whether your brain changes as you get older. [2 marks]

Now try these

The children's answers will be subjective, but should be well justified where appropriate.

Possible answers

1. Open-ended question: Look for accurate definitions of the key or more difficult words in the extract (for example, 'organ', 'cells', 'oxygen', 'bile', 'blood vessels'). The words should be presented alphabetically. [3 marks max]
2. Answers should refer to the text's subheadings, short, concise paragraphs, information box and diagrams/images. [3 marks max]
3. Answers should recognise that subheadings help to organise information, so readers can easily find certain sections they need. They also break up the information, making it clearer and easier for readers to follow. [3 marks max]
4. Open-ended question: Look for relevance to task, imagination, presentation and inclusion of details about how people can look after their brains. [3 marks max]
5. Open-ended question: Look for relevance to task, imagination, presentation and inclusion of facts about the brain. [3 marks max]

Unit 15: Non-fiction (biography): 'Barack Obama'

Overview

English curriculum objectives

- Continue to read and discuss an increasingly wide range of fiction, poetry, plays, non-fiction and reference books or textbooks
- Read books that are structured in different ways and read for a range of purposes
- Identify and discuss themes and conventions in and across a wide range of writing
- Check that the book makes sense to them, discussing their understanding and exploring the meaning of words in context
- Ask questions to improve their understanding
- Summarise the main ideas drawn from more than one paragraph, identifying key details that support the main idea
- Identify how language, structure and presentation contribute to meaning
- Distinguish between statements of fact and opinion
- Retrieve, record and present information from non-fiction
- Participate in discussions about books that are read to them and those they can read for themselves, building on their own and others' ideas and challenging views courteously
- Explain and discuss their understanding of what they have read, including through formal presentations and debates, maintaining a focus on the topic and using notes where necessary
- Provide reasoned justification for their views

Treasure House resources

- Comprehension Skills Pupil Book 5, Unit 15, pages 50–52
- Collins Connect Treasure House Comprehension Year 5, Unit 15
- Photocopiable Unit 15, Resource 1: Questions about the USA, page 113
- Photocopiable Unit 15, Resource 2: Researching civil rights, page 114

Additional resources

- Dictionaries or the internet
- Other examples of biographies (optional)

Introduction

Teaching overview

'Barack Obama' is a non-fiction biography of Barack Hussein Obama, who became the 44th President of the United States of America in 2009. He remained President for eight years. The text provides children with the opportunity to explore a biographical text written in chronological order.

Introduce the text

Ask the children if they know anything about Barack Obama. If they do, invite them to share their knowledge with the class. Then ask what the children know about the form and conventions of biographies, and scribe their ideas on the board.

Tell the children that, in this lesson, they will focus on a non-fiction biographical text about Barack Obama. Then they will answer questions about it. Remind children that sometimes the answers to the questions will be clearly written in the text, but that sometimes they may need to think a little harder and use their own ideas, supported by the text.

Ask the children to read the text individually or in pairs. Ask them to note down any words they do not understand. Discuss unknown or unusual vocabulary before setting children to work answering the questions in the Pupil Book. Try to avoid discussing the content of the text until after the children have answered the questions.

Unit 15: Non-fiction (biography): 'Barack Obama'

Pupil practice

Pupil Book pages 50–52

Get started

Ask children to write sentences to answer the questions, referring to the text where possible.

Suggested answers

1. Barack Obama's date of birth is 4 August 1961. [1 mark]
2. He was born in Honolulu, Hawaii. [1 mark]
3. When he was between five and 10 years old, he lived in Indonesia. [1 mark]
4. He excelled in basketball. [1 mark]
5. Obama noticed that the Christmas catalogues didn't contain anyone of African-American/multiracial heritage like him, and that Santa was a white man. [1 mark]
6. When he was 22 years old, his received the bad news that his father had died in a car accident in Kenya. [1 mark]
7. Obama was elected to the US Senate as a Democrat in 2004. [1 mark]
8. In January 2009, Barack Obama was sworn in as the 44th President of the United States. [1 mark]

Try these

Ask children to write sentences to answer the questions, explaining their answers as fully as they can. The children's answers may be subjective but should be in their own words and well justified, using evidence from either the text or the children's own experiences.

Possible answers

1. Answers should appreciate that a biography is an account of someone's life, and could add that this account should be written by someone else. [2 marks]
2. Answers could refer to features such as factual information presented in a chronological order. The information covers Obama's childhood, his personal life and his career. [2 marks]
3. Answers could suggest readers' interest in American politics, American history, Barack Obama, civil rights, the fact that someone from a complicated background has achieved great things and/or how people become successful. [2 marks]
4. Answers should appreciate the meaning of 'racism' as people's judgements against race (nationality, skin colour, and so on) and the meaning of 'African-American' as referring to someone who identifies themselves as a black American descended from people who originally came from Africa. [2 marks]
5. Answers should refer to the fact that this is the only point at which Obama's own words are reported to the reader, and that the quote marks the point at which Obama starts to realise that his heritage and skin colour are unusual in America (or, at least, in commercial images of the people in America). [2 marks]
6. Answers should refer to a feeling of being 'other' and of unfairness and/or alienation. [2 marks]
7. Answers should attempt to appreciate the difficult decision a mother might face when sending her child away for what she considers to be better 'safety and education'. [2 marks]
8. Open-ended question: Look for relevance to task and justification of choice. [2 marks]

Now try these

The children's answers will be subjective, but should be well justified where appropriate.

Possible answers

1. Answers could refer to Obama's mother's feelings about meeting and marrying Barack Obama Sr, their separation and divorce, meeting and marrying Lolo Soetoro and leaving her home and parents to live in Indonesia; her feelings of fear for her son's safety and education and her decision to send him back to Hawaii; her reunion with her son and grandparents in Hawaii (and her supposed separation from Soetoro); her feelings at the death of Obama Sr; and her feelings of pride at Obama's achievements. [3 marks max]
2. Answers could refer to Obama's intelligence, his sporting talent, his struggle to understand people's perceptions of him, his social consciousness, his unhappiness at his father's absence, his ambition and drive, his choice to work against discrimination and in difficult districts, and his political success. [3 marks max]
3. Open-ended question: Look for six relevant questions directed at Obama that are not answered by the extract, for example: 'How did you feel when your mother sent you back to Hawaii?' 'What made you so determined to succeed?' 'How do you feel about racism in America now?' [3 marks max]
4. Answers should consider the main facts required to write a biography: date and place of birth, family life, childhood and schooling, hobbies, achievements, plans, feelings and any life-changing events. [3 marks max]
5. Answers should show basic understanding about civil rights law (that it is designed to protect against discrimination based on race, gender, and so on), and link Obama's decision to his early experiences of racism, family background and/or his character. [3 marks max]

Unit 15: Non-fiction (biography): 'Barack Obama'

Support, embed & challenge

Support
Support children in understanding more about the content used in a biography. Ask them to write a short biography of their friend's life, first thinking up interview questions and then writing everything down in the correct order.

Embed
Use Unit 15 Resource 1: Questions about the USA to encourage children to consider how specific pieces of information can be found in information texts. The children read two short passages about the USA and then compose three questions about each. Ask pairs to swap questions and answer each other's to check that the questions are relevant to the passages.

Challenge
Use Unit 15 Resource 2: Researching civil rights to challenge children to conduct further research about civil rights. Help children to plan their questions, if required. For example, ask: 'What are civil rights?' 'Why are they important for everyone?' 'Who has fought for civil rights in the USA?' Then ask children to research the answers to their questions and present their findings as either a fact file or a presentation that can be shared with others.

Homework / Additional activities

Best biographies
Ask children to research biographies, and to each find a different new example. The children should note down the subject of the biography they found and what interesting things that person has done. Ask them to be prepared to share and compare their findings with the class or a group.

Collins Connect: Unit 15
Ask the children to complete Unit 15 (see Teach → Year 5 → Comprehension → Unit 15).

Unit 16: Fiction (modern): 'The Hedgehog Mystery'

Overview

English curriculum objectives

- Continue to read and discuss an increasingly wide range of fiction, poetry, plays, non-fiction and reference books or textbooks
- Increase their familiarity with a wide range of books, including myths, legends and traditional stories, modern fiction, fiction from our literary heritage, and books from other cultures and traditions
- Recommend books that they have read to their peers, giving reasons for their choices
- Identify and discuss themes and conventions in and across a wide range of writing
- Make comparisons within and across books
- Check that the book makes sense to them, discussing their understanding and exploring the meaning of words in context
- Ask questions to improve their understanding
- Draw inferences such as inferring characters' feelings, thoughts and motives from their actions, and justifying inferences with evidence
- Predict what might happen from details stated and implied
- Identify how language, structure and presentation contribute to meaning
- Discuss and evaluate how authors use language, including figurative language, considering the impact on the reader
- Participate in discussions about books that are read to them and those they can read for themselves, building on their own and others' ideas and challenging views courteously
- Explain and discuss their understanding of what they have read, including through formal presentations and debates, maintaining a focus on the topic and using notes where necessary
- Provide reasoned justification for their views

Treasure House resources

- Comprehension Skills Pupil Book 5, Unit 16, pages 53–55
- Photocopiable Unit 16, Resource 1: Mum and Gran, page 115
- Photocopiable Unit 16, Resource 2: Gang rules, page 116

Additional resources

- Dictionaries or the internet
- *The Hedgehog Mystery* by Ally Kennen, whole text (optional)

Introduction

Teaching overview

The Hedgehog Mystery is a humorous mystery story about two children, Ellie and Morris, and their Gran. Gran is a red-haired, leather-jacket-wearing motorbike gang member – but also 'the softest old bird ever'. The extract introduces the characters and gives children the opportunity to examine how their personalities are established. Later in the story, Gran's lodger disappears with her motorbike and the children decide to take matters into their own hands.

Introduce the extract

Ask the children if any of them have read the story *The Hedgehog Mystery*. If they have, invite them to share their knowledge with the class. Then ask the children to remind you about the characteristics of mystery stories.

Tell the children that, in this lesson, they will focus on one extract from the beginning of a mystery story. Then they will answer questions about it. Remind children that sometimes the answers to the questions will be clearly written in the extract, but that sometimes they may need to think a little harder and use their own ideas, supported by the text.

Ask the children to read the extract individually or in pairs. Ask them to note down any words they do not understand. Discuss unknown or unusual vocabulary before setting children to work answering the questions in the Pupil Book. Try to avoid discussing the content of the extract until after the children have answered the questions.

Unit 16: Fiction (modern): 'The Hedgehog Mystery'

Pupil practice

Pupil Book pages 53–55

Get started

Ask children to write sentences to answer the questions, referring to the text where possible.

Suggested answers

1. Gran's motorbike is jet black with orange flames painted down the sides. [1 mark]
2. Gran calls her motorbike 'Fenella'. [1 mark]
3. Gran keeps her motorbike chained up in her front garden. [1 mark]
4. Gran has dyed red hair, wears a leather jacket with a hedgehog painted on the back and wears lots of silver rings. [2 marks]
5. Gran has a hedgehog painted on the back of her jacket because she is part of a gang called the 'Hedgehogs'. [1 mark]
6. Mum dislikes Gran's motorbike: she says that 'sixty-two year old grandmothers shouldn't ride motorbikes'. [1 mark]
7. Gran defends Mum's behaviour by saying that it is because she loves them so much, and that she's only trying to look after them. [1 mark]
8. Morris is the speaker's younger brother. [1 mark]

Try these

Ask children to write sentences to answer the questions, explaining their answers as fully as they can. The children's answers may be subjective but should be in their own words and well justified, using evidence from either the text or the children's own experiences.

Possible answers

1. Answers should grasp that the phrase 'goes like stink' means 'goes really quickly'. [2 marks]
2. Answers could suggest that Mum is disapproving of Gran's behaviour only because she cares about Gran and doesn't want her to be hurt, because she worries that Gran will be a bad influence on the children and/or because she is embarrassed by the impression Gran makes. [2 marks]
3. Answers should detect that the sentence 'And one day, horribly, she turns out to be right' warns the reader that something bad is going to happen. [2 marks]
4. Answers should conclude that the narrator is still annoyed by her mother, as the sentences 'she can be a right pain' and 'I get annoyed with Mum sometimes' are in the present tense.

5. Answers should infer that Gran plays a big part of the family's life. She lives in the house opposite her daughter and grandchildren, and she looks after the children every day after school while their mother works. [2 marks]
6. Answers could suggest that Gran was standing on her head because she was practising yoga (or exercising in another way) or that she was simply enjoying it. [2 marks]
7. Answers could detect that the speaker is very fond of Gran. She describes her in admiring tones, seems to agree with Gran's attitude more than Mum's and refers to her as 'the softest old bird ever'. [2 marks]
8. Answers should detect that this is a modern story because it contains references to a motorbike and 'the telly'. [2 marks]

Now try these

The children's answers will be subjective, but should be well justified where appropriate.

Possible answers

1. Answers could refer to Gran's modern interests, youthful attitude, liveliness, quirkiness, sense of fun, outgoing nature, sympathy for Mum's attitudes and affection for her grandchildren. [3 marks max]
2. Answers should detect that the reader is able to engage with the characters and the story quickly because the author immediately and effectively describes the characters, and then gets the story moving promptly, explaining where the characters are and what they are doing. [3 marks max]
3. Answers could refer to the speaker's admiration and affection for Gran, criticism of and irritation with Mum, acknowledgement that Mum's fears prove to be right, anticipation of arriving at Gran's after school, consideration of her brother Morris, and eventual friendly interaction with Gran. [3 marks max]
4. Answers should detect that the sentence 'Every day, after school, me and my brother Morris go to Gran's' marks a change in the story because, before this point, the author is setting the scene by describing the characters of Gran and Mum. After this sentence, the author describes the action as the plot progresses. [3 marks max]
5. Open-ended question: Look for relevance to task, consistency of character and theme, imagination and presentation. [3 marks max]

Support, embed & challenge

Support
Support children in understanding the content and perspective of the extract by asking them to rewrite part of it in the third person. Point out that the extract is currently being written by Morris's sister. Ask them to write out the end section (from 'Every day, after school') as an independent narrator, modelling the process first if necessary.

Embed
Use Unit 16 Resource 1: Mum and Gran to encourage children to write a dialogue between Gran and Mum in which Mum is trying to persuade Gran to give up her motorbike. Ask them to reread the extract carefully to gather information about each woman's character and what they may say.

Challenge
Challenge children to use Unit 16 Resource 2: Gang rules to create some gang rules for the 'Hedgehogs'. Encourage them to use the information in the extract and their imaginations.

Homework / Additional activities

Is Gran too old?
Ask children to write arguments for either side of the debate question: 'Is Gran too old to ride a motorbike?' Then ask them to write a paragraph each, giving their conclusions and personal opinions.

Unit 17: Fiction (traditional tale): 'The Dragon Pearl'

Overview

English curriculum objectives

- Continue to read and discuss an increasingly wide range of fiction, poetry, plays, non-fiction and reference books or textbooks
- Increase their familiarity with a wide range of books, including myths, legends and traditional stories, modern fiction, fiction from our literary heritage, and books from other cultures and traditions
- Recommend books that they have read to their peers, giving reasons for their choices
- Identify and discuss themes and conventions in and across a wide range of writing
- Make comparisons within and across books
- Check that the book makes sense to them, discussing their understanding and exploring the meaning of words in context
- Ask questions to improve their understanding
- Draw inferences such as inferring characters' feelings, thoughts and motives from their actions, and justifying inferences with evidence
- Predict what might happen from details stated and implied
- Identify how language, structure and presentation contribute to meaning
- Discuss and evaluate how authors use language, including figurative language, considering the impact on the reader
- Participate in discussions about books that are read to them and those they can read for themselves, building on their own and others' ideas and challenging views courteously
- Explain and discuss their understanding of what they have read, including through formal presentations and debates, maintaining a focus on the topic and using notes where necessary
- Provide reasoned justification for their views

Treasure House resources

- Comprehension Skills Pupil Book 5, Unit 17, pages 56–58
- Photocopiable Unit 17, Resource 1: The magical pearl, page 117
- Photocopiable Unit 17, Resource 2: The start of the story, page 118

Additional resources

- Dictionaries or the internet
- *Two Dragon Tales* by Dawn Casey, whole text (optional)

Introduction

Teaching overview

'The Dragon Pearl' is a traditional tale about a poor Chinese boy, Xiao Sheng, who lives with his poor mother. When the extract begins, Xiao Sheng and his mother have become wealthy, as they have come to possess a dragon's pearl that grants them everything they could possibly need. The extract describes the exciting point at which, swallowing the pearl to try and hide it, Xiao Sheng is transformed into a dragon. It encourages children to draw inferences regarding characters' feelings, thoughts and motives from their actions, and to justify inferences with evidence. There are opportunities to develop children's ability to evaluate how authors use language to portray characters' feelings, thoughts and motives, considering the impact on the reader.

Introduce the extract

Ask the children to help you recall the features of traditional tales (such as a problem, quest and solution). Take suggestions and scribe them on the board.

Tell the children that, in this lesson, they will focus on one extract from a traditional tale called 'The Dragon Pearl'. Then they will answer questions about it. Remind children that sometimes the answers to the questions will be clearly written in the extract, but that sometimes they may need to think a little harder and use their own ideas, supported by the text.

Ask the children to read the extract individually or in pairs. Ask them to note down any words they do not understand. Discuss unknown or unusual vocabulary before setting children to work answering the questions in the Pupil Book. Try to avoid discussing the content of the extract until after the children have answered the questions.

Pupil practice

Pupil Book pages 56–58

Get started

Ask children to write sentences to answer the questions, referring to the text where possible.

Suggested answers

1. Xiao Sheng and his mother now had plenty of everything. [1 mark]
2. Lord Zhou, the landlord, was banging on the door. [1 mark]
3. The magic item Xiao Sheng had was a pearl. [1 mark]
4. Xiao Sheng's mother went pale because she was frightened. [1 mark]
5. Xiao Sheng put the pearl in his mouth (and then accidentally swallowed it). [1 mark]
6. In Xiao Sheng's belly, the pearl felt like a burning ball of fire. [2 marks]
7. Xiao Sheng drained (drank) all the tea in the pot. [1 mark]
8. Xiao Sheng's body began to change. (Steam poured from his nose; scales rippled down his back; antlers sprouted through his hair. It became a dragon's body.) [1 mark]

Try these

Ask children to write sentences to answer the questions, explaining their answers as fully as they can. The children's answers may be subjective but should be in their own words and well justified, using evidence from either the text or the children's own experiences.

Possible answers

1. Answers should detect that the opening line, 'Now Xiao Sheng and his mother had plenty of everything'", suggests that the extract is not from the beginning of the story. The extract ends on a dramatic and unresolved change (Xiao Sheng transforming into a dragon), which suggests that this is not the end of the tale. [2 marks]
2. Answers should detect that Xiao Sheng made sure that everyone in the village was provided for because the people of the village had always been good to Xiao Sheng and his mother. [2 marks]
3. Answers should detect that, if it weren't for Xiao Sheng, the villagers wouldn't have enough to eat because the rains didn't fall and the crops didn't grow. [2 marks]
4. Answers should discern that Xiao Sheng and his mother had not always had plenty of everything because of the word 'now' in the first sentence. They could then (correctly) deduce that the magic pearl is the reason that they now have everything they need because it is referred to as 'magic' and highly desired by others. [2 marks]
5. Answers could refer to Xiao Sheng's lack of fear, defiance, bravery and/or mild hostility with regards to Lord Zhou. [2 marks]
6. Answers could refer to Xiao Sheng's mother's pride, gratitude, concern and love with regards to her son. [2 marks]
7. The author suggests that Xiao Sheng turning into a dragon is a beautiful rather than horrific process by using the words 'brilliant' to describe his scales, 'magnificent' to describe his antlers and 'mighty' to describe his head. [2 marks]
8. Answers may suggest that the pearl belonged to Xiao Sheng and his mother, to 'everyone' (as stated by Xiao Sheng in the extract), possibly to Lord Zhou or to a dragon. Answers should be justified. [2 marks]

Now try these

The children's answers will be subjective, but should be well justified where appropriate.

Possible answers

1. Answers could refer to Xiao Sheng's kindness in providing for the villagers, his bravery in standing up to Lord Zhou and his quick thinking/impulsiveness in swallowing the pearl. [2 marks]
2. Answers could refer to Xiao Sheng's mother's pride or generosity as she and her son provided for the villagers, alarm at Lord Zhou's knock, fear of Lord Zhou, worry for her son and wonder/shock/astonishment/awe as she sees him turn into a dragon. [2 marks]
3. Answers should identify that Xiao Sheng looked at his mother with 'wide eyes', which suggests that he did not intend to swallow the pearl. They could also refer to Lord Zhou shaking him unexpectedly while the pearl was in his mouth and his alarm at the effects he experiences once the pearl is swallowed. [3 marks max]
4. Answers may refer to Xiao Sheng's initial physical discomfort, alarm and shock at his transformation, loss of his old life with his mother and/or appreciation of what he will be able to do as a dragon. [3 marks max]
5. Open-ended question: Look for relevance to task, consistency of character and theme, imagination and presentation. Answers could detect that the dragon blows out 'cloud after billowing cloud' and that this could solve the villagers' problems when the clouds cause rain to fall and crops can grow. [3 marks max]

Unit 17: Fiction (traditional tale): 'The Dragon Pearl'

Support, embed & challenge

Support
Use Unit 17 Resource 1: The magical pearl to support children in understanding the properties of the magical pearl by answering the questions using details from the extract.

Embed
Use Unit 17 Resource 2: The start of the story to encourage children to consider what must have happened before the extract begins. Ask them to use the planning grid to structure their thoughts and then to write the start of the story.

Challenge
Challenge the children to rewrite the extract from the perspective of Lord Zhou. Encourage them to 'step into the shoes' of Lord Zhou, and to embrace the idea that he might genuinely feel entitled to the pearl.

Homework / Additional activities

Write a similar tale
Ask children to write a tale with a similar story line to 'The Dragon Pearl'. Think about what the pearl could be substituted for and who the characters might be. Ask children to think about which elements of the story they would change and which they would keep the same.

Unit 18: Poetry: 'What on Earth?' and 'Progress Man!'

Overview

English curriculum objectives

- Continue to read and discuss an increasingly wide range of fiction, poetry, plays, non-fiction and reference books or textbooks
- Identify and discuss themes and conventions in and across a wide range of writing
- Learn a wider range of poetry by heart
- Prepare poems and plays to read aloud and to perform, showing understanding through intonation, tone and volume so that the meaning is clear to an audience
- Check that the book makes sense to them, discussing their understanding and exploring the meaning of words in context
- Ask questions to improve their understanding
- Draw inferences such as inferring characters' feelings, thoughts and motives from their actions, and justifying inferences with evidence
- Identify how language, structure and presentation contribute to meaning
- Discuss and evaluate how authors use language, including figurative language, considering the impact on the reader
- Participate in discussions about books that are read to them and those they can read for themselves, building on their own and others' ideas and challenging views courteously
- Explain and discuss their understanding of what they have read, including through formal presentations and debates, maintaining a focus on the topic and using notes where necessary
- Provide reasoned justification for their views

Treasure House resources

- Comprehension Skills Pupil Book 5, Unit 18, pages 59–61
- Photocopiable Unit 18, Resource 1: Comparing the poems, page 119
- Photocopiable Unit 18, Resource 2: My progress poem, page 120

Additional resources

- Dictionaries or the internet
- Other poems about the environment (optional)

Introduction

Teaching overview

'What on Earth?' and 'Progress Man!' are both poems by Judith Nicholls. Each deals with the problems caused to the environment by urban expansion and progress. 'What on Earth?' shows how rhetorical questions can be used in writing, and 'Progress Man!' presents a good example of personification.

Introduce the poems

Ask the children if any of them know of any local building developments, such as new houses or new commercial premises. If they do, invite them to share their knowledge with the class. Then ask them to consider how big building projects can affect people, and how they can affect the environment.

Tell the children that, in this lesson, they will focus on two poems about how progress affects the environment. Then they will answer questions about it. Remind children that sometimes the answers to the questions will be clearly written in the poems, but that sometimes they may need to think a little harder and use their own ideas, supported by the text.

Ask the children to read the poems individually or in pairs. Ask them to note down any words they do not understand. Discuss unknown or unusual vocabulary before setting children to work answering the questions in the Pupil Book. Try to avoid discussing the content of the poems until after the children have answered the questions.

Unit 18: Poetry: 'What on Earth?' and 'Progress Man!'

Pupil practice

Pupil Book pages 59–61

Get started

Ask children to write sentences to answer the questions, referring to the text where possible.

Suggested answers

1. Wood-pigeons flew where oak and ash grew. [1 mark]
2. A whining grey plane flies through the forest now. [1 mark]
3. Blackberries once hung at the end of the lane. [1 mark]
4. The lane has become a car park. [1 mark]
5. Progress Man says we need a motorway. [1 mark]
6. Progress Man's response to being told that we have some roads already is: 'Well, not enough, I say'. [1 mark]
7. Progress Man says a little drop of oil spilt over golden sand is a tiny price to pay. [1 mark]
8. Progress man says that the world has 'so much' land. [1 mark]

Try these

Ask children to write sentences to answer the questions, explaining their answers as fully as they can. The children's answers may be subjective but should be in their own words and well justified, using evidence from either the text or the children's own experiences.

Possible answers

1. Answers should deduce that the poet is trying to convey the message that the development of new roads and buildings destroys natural landscapes. [2 marks]
2. Answers should deduce that the poet is trying to convey the message that progress is an impatient, strong-willed and destructive process. [2 marks]
3. Answers should detect that the speaker in 'Progress Man!' is Progress Man himself (except for the words 'cried Progress'). [2 marks]
4. Answers should deduce that the 'we' mentioned in both poems is the human race. [2 marks]
5. Answers should explain that the rhyming patterns are similar because both poems follow the pattern ABCB. [2 marks]
6. Answers should conclude that the line 'the forest's a runway' is meant literally: the forest was cut down and an airport was built on the land. [2 marks]
7. Answers should detect that the concept of progress becoming 'Progress Man' is an example of personification. [2 marks]
8. Open-ended question: Look for reasonable justifications for the preference stated. [2 marks]

Now try these

The children's answers will be subjective, but should be well justified where appropriate.

Possible answers

1. Answers should be in the children's own words, and may refer to similarities in the structure and form of the poems (each has six stanzas of four lines, each with the rhyming pattern ABCB), and their similarity in theme. [3 marks max]
2. Answers should be in the children's own words, and may refer to differences such as the attitudes and speakers of the poems: in 'What on Earth?', the speaker is a person upset by the developments described; in 'Progress Man!', the speaker is progress itself, and is therefore enthusiastic about the changes described. [3 marks max]
3. Answers may refer to Progress Man's confidence, strong-mindedness, determination, disregard for the environment and dismissal of the environmental objections mentioned. [3 marks max]
4. The word 'progress' can be defined as a verb or a noun, in both cases meaning 'moving forwards'. Answers may conclude that 'Progress Man' represents an actual man (for example, a developer), or that he represents the concept of progress. Either answer should be well justified. [3 marks max]
5. Open-ended question: Look for relevance to task, consistency of style and theme, imagination and presentation. [3 marks max]

Unit 18: Poetry: 'What on Earth?' and 'Progress Man!'

Support, embed & challenge

Support
Use Unit 18 Resource 1: Comparing the poems to support children in analysing and comparing the poems' content, messages and presentation.

Embed
Use Unit 18 Resource 2: My progress poem to encourage children to explore the composition of 'Progress Man!' by replacing some of its key elements with ideas of their own. If children find they can achieve this task, they could then continue their new version of the poem, using the text for guidance.

Challenge
Challenge children to write a poem in response to 'Progress Man!', from the perspective of Conservation Man. Suggest that they use the structure of the original for guidance.

Homework / Additional activities

What issues affect your area?
Ask children to conduct research into any local environmental issues. Support them by suggesting they look in the local newspaper or on a council website, and search for issues such as planning and development and waste management.

Unit 19: Non-fiction (information text): 'How to be an Ancient Greek in 25 easy stages'

Overview

English curriculum objectives

- Continue to read and discuss an increasingly wide range of fiction, poetry, plays, non-fiction and reference books or textbooks
- Read books that are structured in different ways and read for a range of purposes
- Identify and discuss themes and conventions in and across a wide range of writing
- Check that the book makes sense to them, discussing their understanding and exploring the meaning of words in context
- Ask questions to improve their understanding
- Summarise the main ideas drawn from more than one paragraph, identifying key details that support the main idea
- Identify how language, structure and presentation contribute to meaning
- Distinguish between statements of fact and opinion
- Retrieve, record and present information from non-fiction
- Participate in discussions about books that are read to them and those they can read for themselves, building on their own and others' ideas and challenging views courteously
- Explain and discuss their understanding of what they have read, including through formal presentations and debates, maintaining a focus on the topic and using notes where necessary
- Provide reasoned justification for their views

Treasure House resources

- Comprehension Skills Pupil Book 5, Unit 19, pages 62–64
- Photocopiable Unit 19, Resource 1: Quick quiz, page 121
- Photocopiable Unit 19, Resource 2: Ancient instructions, page 122

Additional resources

- Dictionaries or the internet
- *How to be an Ancient Greek in 25 easy stages* by Scoular Anderson, whole text (optional)

Introduction

Teaching overview

How to be an Ancient Greek in 25 easy stages is a fun, accessible information text exploring the lives and times of the Ancient Greeks. In the extract, the children read 'Stage 3: Go from riches to rags' and 'Stage 4: Make your voice heard'. The text features subheadings and labelled diagrams as well as factual explanations.

Introduce the extract

Ask the children if any of them have any knowledge of what life was like for people living in Ancient Greece. If they have, invite them to share their knowledge with the class.

Tell the children that, in this lesson, they will focus on one extract from an information text about what it was like to be an Ancient Greek. Then they will answer questions about it. Remind children that sometimes the answers to the questions will be clearly written in the extract, but that sometimes they may need to think a little harder and use their own ideas, supported by the text.

Ask the children to read the extract individually or in pairs. Ask them to note down any words they do not understand. Discuss unknown or unusual vocabulary before setting children to work answering the questions in the Pupil Book. Try to avoid discussing the content of the extract until after the children have answered the questions.

Pupil practice

Unit 19: Non-fiction (information text): 'How to be an Ancient Greek in 25 easy stages'

Pupil Book pages 62–64

Get started

Ask children to write sentences to answer the questions, referring to the text where possible.

Suggested answers

1. If you were born a Mycenaean king who had just died, you would be buried with large amounts of gold and jewellery, and your weapons, armour and shield. [1 mark]
2. The Mycenaean people are described as being wealthy and warlike. [1 mark]
3. The image tells you that the four objects that were found in Mycenaean graves were a gold mask (placed over the face of a dead king), a bronze suit of armour, shields and a pot painted with an octopus design. [1 mark]
4. In the centre of each kingdom in Ancient Greece was a polis/city. [1 mark]
5. The word 'acropolis' means high city. [1 mark]
6. The Mycenaean civilisation lasted for a few hundred years. [1 mark]
7. During the Dark Ages, the Greeks forgot how to read and write. [1 mark]
8. According to the extract, Athene was a goddess who gave her name to the city of Athens. [1 mark]

Try these

Ask children to write sentences to answer the questions, explaining their answers as fully as they can. The children's answers may be subjective but should be in their own words and well justified, using evidence from either the text or the children's own experiences.

Possible answers

1. Answers should state that the Mycenaeans left their cities to crumble because they migrated to other lands to escape starvation. [2 marks]
2. Answers could suggest that the city of Athens moved downhill because it became less vulnerable to attack and so needed its defensive position less, because the non-sacred elements of the city were prioritised less than the temples, or for any practical reason (such as the availability of water in the valley and/or the ease of not climbing the hill). [2 marks]
3. The image of Athens gives the reader a visual guide to the positions of the temples of Athens and the defensive wall around them, labelling and locating the Acropolis, Parthenon, Propylaea, temple of Athene Nike and a huge bronze statue of Athene. It also explains the meanings of the terms 'propylaea' (gateway) and 'nike' (victorious). [2 marks]
4. Open-ended question: The child's choice should be justified. [2 marks]
5. Answers could suggest that readers may want to read this text to learn about Ancient Greek life or any specific aspect(s) of it. [2 marks]
6. Answers could conclude that it is important for us to understand about people and culture from history so that we have a sense of human progression, so we can learn from past mistakes and/or in order to broaden our experiences and consider new ideas. They may otherwise assert that it is not important for us to understand about people and culture from history, perhaps because ancient history has little relevance to modern life. [2 marks]
7. Open-ended question: Answers could mention the Athenians' liking for music, poetry and the theatre, and/or their regular state of war. [2 marks]
8. Answers should recognise that the author is likely to have conducted thorough research about Ancient Greece in order to write the book. [2 marks]

Now try these

The children's answers will be subjective, but should be well justified where appropriate.

Possible answers

1. Open-ended question: Look for accurate definitions of the key or more difficult words in the extract (for example, 'acropolis', 'civilisation', 'migrated', 'fortified'). The words should be presented alphabetically. [3 marks max]
2. Answers should refer to the text's subheadings, diagrams/illustrations, clear paragraphs and historical facts. [3 marks max]
3. Answers could suggest that the different stages are used to help separate different topics, to assist the reader in navigating the text and to break it up into easier-to-read sections. [3 marks max]
4. Open-ended question: Look for relevance to task, imagination, presentation and inclusion of details about the polis of Athens from the text. [3 marks max]
5. Open-ended question: Look for relevance to task, imagination, presentation and inclusion of details about Ancient Greek cities from the text or elsewhere. [3 marks max]

Unit 19: Non-fiction (information text): 'How to be an Ancient Greek in 25 easy stages'

Support, embed & challenge

Support
Use Unit 19 Resource 1: Quick quiz to support children in grounding the knowledge they have gained from the extract as they create a short quiz on it. Ask children to come up with five questions that the extract can answer, and then swap their quiz with a partner.

Embed
Use Unit 19 Resource 2: Ancient instructions to encourage children to consider the information in the extract in detail. Point out that the subheadings in the extract are instructions, but that most of the text is an explanation. Ask children to convert one paragraph of explanation into five simple instructions.

Suggestions for appropriate paragraphs (also given on the worksheet) are:
- how to construct a polis
- what the Mycenaeans should do after the long period of bad weather
- things Athenians could do for fun.

Challenge
Challenge children to research and create a short presentation about another ancient civilisation: the Aztecs, Ancient Romans, Ancient Britons or Ancient Egyptians. Ask them to be prepared to share their presentation with the class or a group.

Homework / Additional activities

More about the Mycenaeans
Ask children to research more about the Mycenaeans. Ask children to prepare a list of six questions they would like to know about the Mycenaean people and then try to research and find the answers. Ask them to refer to the structure and style of the extract to help them write their reports.

Unit 20: Non-fiction (autobiography): 'Ade Adepitan: A Paralympian's Story'

Overview

English curriculum objectives

- Continue to read and discuss an increasingly wide range of fiction, poetry, plays, non-fiction and reference books or textbooks
- Read books that are structured in different ways and read for a range of purposes
- Identify and discuss themes and conventions in and across a wide range of writing
- Check that the book makes sense to them, discussing their understanding and exploring the meaning of words in context
- Ask questions to improve their understanding
- Summarise the main ideas drawn from more than one paragraph, identifying key details that support the main idea
- Identify how language, structure and presentation contribute to meaning
- Distinguish between statements of fact and opinion
- Retrieve, record and present information from non-fiction
- Participate in discussions about books that are read to them and those they can read for themselves, building on their own and others' ideas and challenging views courteously
- Explain and discuss their understanding of what they have read, including through formal presentations and debates, maintaining a focus on the topic and using notes where necessary
- Provide reasoned justification for their views

Treasure House resources

- Comprehension Skills Pupil Book 5, Unit 20, pages 65–67
- Photocopiable Unit 20, Resource 1: Ade's reasons, page 123
- Photocopiable Unit 20, Resource 2: Fact or opinion? page 124

Additional resources

- Dictionaries or the internet
- *Ade Adepitan: A Paralympian's Story* by Ade Adepitan, whole text (optional)

Introduction

Teaching overview

Ade Adepitan: A Paralympian's Story is an autobiographical text by the Paralympian medal winner, commentator and successful TV presenter Ade Adepitan. In the extract, Ade tells about his memories of starting to play basketball. The text provides children with the opportunity to explore an autobiographical text written in chronological order, with content that children may be able to relate to.

Introduce the extract

Ask the children if they have any prior knowledge of Ade Adepitan. If they do, invite them to share their knowledge with the class. If not, use the information in the 'Teaching overview' above to explain who he is.

Tell the children that, in this lesson, they will focus on one extract from Ade's autobiography. Then they will answer questions about it. Remind children that sometimes the answers to the questions will be clearly written in the extract, but that sometimes they may need to think a little harder and use their own ideas, supported by the text.

Ask the children to read the extract individually or in pairs. Ask them to note down any words they do not understand. Discuss unknown or unusual vocabulary before setting children to work answering the questions in the Pupil Book. Try to avoid discussing the content of the extract until after the children have answered the questions.

Unit 20: Non-fiction (autobiography): 'Ade Adepitan: A Paralympian's Story'

Pupil practice

Pupil Book pages 65–67

Get started

Ask children to write sentences to answer the questions, referring to the text where possible.

Suggested answers

1. Ade was about 12 or 13 years old when he started playing basketball. [1 mark]
2. His first wheelchair basketball team was called the Newham Rollers. [1 mark]
3. Ade describes the GB players as really big, with massive arms; he says they looked like athletes and were 'so cool'. [1 mark]
4. The GB players' wheelchairs were different from ordinary wheelchairs because they were state-of-the-art funky wheelchairs. [1 mark]
5. The precise moment at which Ade decided he wanted to be like the GB basketball team players was when, as they were going past, one of them gave him a wink. [1 mark]
6. When he first sat in the basketball wheelchair, Ade felt like the basketball was the same size as him. [1 mark]
7. When Ade first played in the junior championships, they lost. [1 mark]
8. When Ade returned to the tournament the following year, they reached the final. [1 mark]

Try these

Ask children to write sentences to answer the questions, explaining their answers as fully as they can. The children's answers may be subjective but should be in their own words and well justified, using evidence from either the text or the children's own experiences.

Possible answers

1. Answers should recognise that an autobiography is a life story written by the person who is its subject. [2 marks]
2. Answers should identify the features of a narrative written in the first person, of the author being the subject, of life events being described and of the facts being presented in chronological order. [2 marks]
3. Answers could suggest that people might be interested in learning about who Ade is, what he has achieved and how he has achieved his successes. [2 marks]
4. Answers could suggest that Ade's strong sense of pride is linked to him overcoming his difficulties through hard work, and possibly to him wanting to prove himself – to himself as much as to anyone else (he says he didn't really think of himself as being disabled). [2 marks]
5. Answers could suggest that the fact stated (that Ade was having therapy to help him to walk before getting a basketball wheelchair) might help to explain how he felt about wheelchairs because he was trying very hard not to use them, and because using one may have felt like giving up. [2 marks]
6. Answers could suggest that his parents may have felt disappointed that Ade was using a wheelchair instead of continuing therapy, and/or that they were glad to see him engaging in a new team sport. [2 marks]
7. Answers should recognise that Ade's perception of wheelchairs changed positively over time: he went from thinking of them as ugly and unhelpful to seeing them as funky and athletic, and a useful tool. [2 marks]
8. Open-ended question: The child's choice of Ade's experiences should be justified. [2 marks]

Now try these

The children's answers will be subjective, but should be well justified where appropriate.

Possible answers

1. Answers could include Ade's school friends' sadness that he couldn't play football with them, hope that his therapy will work, gladness when he finds a sport he enjoys, possible envy at him meeting GB players, possible sadness as he spends more time away from them playing basketball, disappointment for him when he loses the junior championships and pride when he reaches the finals the following year. [3 marks max]
2. Answers could refer to Ade's determination, pride, sporty nature, admiration of the GB basketball wheelchair players, adventurous and positive spirit, strong work ethic and willingness to change his opinions. [3 marks max]
3. Open-ended question: Look for six relevant questions directed at Ade that are not answered by the extract, for example: 'Where did you grow up?' 'What are your earliest memories of school?' 'What has been the most significant event in your life so far?' [3 marks max]
4. Answers should consider the main facts required to write an autobiography: date and place of birth, family life, childhood and schooling, hobbies, achievements, plans, feelings and any life-changing events. [3 marks max]
5. Open-ended question: Look for relevance to task, reference to details given in the extract, imagination and presentation. [3 marks max]

Unit 20: Non-fiction (autobiography): 'Ade Adepitan: A Paralympian's Story'

Support, embed & challenge

Support
Use Unit 20 Resource 1: Ade's reasons to support children in finding the feelings and opinions that lie behind the facts of Ade Adepitan's life. Ask them to locate each fact in the extract, and help them to read around it to find a reason why Ade acted as he did.

Embed
Use Unit 20 Resource 2: Fact or opinion? to encourage children to consider the personal and impersonal elements of an autobiography. Ask them to read through the text again and sort the information into two columns: 'Facts' or 'Opinions and feelings'.

Challenge
Challenge children to write short autobiographies of their own lives so far. Ask them to plan what information they will write about and make notes in chronological order. Remind them to use a combination of facts and their own feelings and opinions.

Homework / Additional activities

My future
Ask children to write a short report about their hopes for the future. Ask: 'What would you like your autobiography to contain when you are much older?' Encourage children to think about their hopes, dreams and wishes, and how they might fulfil some of these.

Review unit 3: Poetry: 'Summer Afternoon' and 'Gathering in the Days'   Pupil Book pages 68–69

Get started
Ask children to write sentences to answer the questions, referring to the text where possible.

Suggested answers

1. The mud cakes are drying in the farmyard. [1 mark]
2. The clouds have 'died a death': they have gone. [1 mark]
3. The shimmering tarmac is compared to water. [1 mark]
4. The dogs can hear bumblebees humming. [1 mark]
5. The speaker's grandad was on the hillside scything hay. [1 mark]
6. In the afternoons, the speaker's grandmother sleeps beside the fireplace. [1 mark]
7. A boy and a girl were playing in the orchard. [1 mark]
8. The speaker's mother is standing at a window, looking and smiling at the family outside, as she gathers in the day. [1 mark]

Try these
Ask children to write sentences to answer the questions, explaining their answers as fully as they can. The children's answers may be subjective but should be in their own words and well justified, using evidence from either the text or the children's own experiences.

Possible answers

1. Answers should conclude that the weather in 'Summer Afternoon' is very hot and still. It is hot enough to make mud cakes dry out, disperse the clouds, make the tarmac look as if it is shimmering and prompt the cows to stand in the stream. The air is described as holding its breath. [2 marks]
2. Answers should detect that the weather in 'Gathering in the Days' is warm and sunny, but cool enough for the speaker's grandmother to have lit a fire. The speaker's grandad wipes his brow, his grandmother stirs a fire's embers in the afternoon, and all the people mentioned shared the 'selfsame sun'. [2 marks]
3. Answers should recognise that the cows are standing in the stream to cool down. [2 marks]
4. Answers should identify that the rhyming pattern in each verse of both poems is ABCB. [2 marks]
5. Answers should identify that each line in 'Summer Afternoon' contain three stressed beats. The first three lines the verses in 'Gathering in the Days' each contain four beats, and the final line contains three.
6. Answers should conclude that both poems seem to portray positive emotions. Despite the fact that 'Summer Afternoon' includes the negative words 'died' and 'death', the imagery generated by dogs falling asleep, bumblebees cruising and cows in the stream is calm and relaxing. In 'Gathering in the Days', the speaker is reminiscing fondly about his family. Images created by phrases such as 'screams of laughter' and 'lifts her eyes and smiles' are positive. [2 marks]
7. Examples of personification in the poems are: 'The clouds have died a death', 'The air is holding its breath' and 'cruising bumblebees'. Answers need suggest only one. [2 marks]
8. Answers should infer that 'gathering in the day' means something approximating 'soaking up / absorbing what is going on around them', perhaps as if to create a mental picture for future reference. [2 marks]

Now try these
The children's answers will be subjective, but should be well justified where appropriate.

Possible answers

1. Answers may refer to similarities in the structure and form of the poems' verses, and/or in their themes and attitudes. [3 marks max]
2. Answers may refer to differences such as the more personal nature of 'Gathering in the Days' and/or the length of the poems. [3 marks max]
3. Answers could refer to the speaker's fondness for his family, observant nature, appreciation of nature and mindfulness of a moment in time. [3 marks max]
4. Answers should mention the final verse's reference to all the people the poet remembers, which unites the people mentioned in the previous verses. They could also mention that the phrase 'gathering in the day' is repeated a final time, creating a sense of continuity. [3 marks max]
5. Open-ended question: Look for relevance to task, consistency of style and theme, imagination and presentation. [3 marks max]

Unit 1 Resource 1

How the thief was caught

Imagine you are the guilty servant. Fill in the table below to show what you think at each point in the story.

You have been stealing from the rich man.

The rich man has discovered someone has been stealing.

The rich man has explained his plan.

You are about to enter the dark room.

The rich man has caught you!

Unit 1 Resource 2

Servants' speech

Imagine that two of the servants are talking to each other as they wait to enter the dark room. One of them is guilty and the other is innocent. What would they say to one another?

Unit 2 Resource 1

Inside or outside?

Find all the descriptions of the chicken shed and the outside world in the text, and add them to the correct column.

Then link the descriptions to show direct comparisons. For example, link how the inside of the shed smelled to how the outside world smelled.

Inside the shed	Outside the shed

Unit 2 Resource 2

A dippy comic strip

Retell the extract as a comic strip. Look carefully at the number of panels in the template, and where the thought and speech bubbles are placed.

Unit 3 Resource 1

Robinson Crusoe's character

Use the text and your own ideas to create a character profile of Robinson Crusoe.

Picture	Name
	Age
Family details	
Physical description	**Personality**
Likes	**Dislikes**

Unit 3 Resource 2

Other days' diaries

Write two more diary extracts as though you are Robinson Crusoe.

Firstly, write the entry that describes the storm and the shipwreck.

Then write the diary entry for the day after the one in the extract. What will Crusoe do next?

First day

Ninth day

Unit 4 Resource 1

Finding the facts

Fill in the facts by finding the information in 'Cubs and Brownies to the rescue'.

What happened?	
When did it happen?	
Where did it happen?	
Why did it happen?	
How did it happen?	
Who was involved?	
What did the people interviewed say?	
How did they feel?	

Unit 4 Resource 2

A new news report

Imagine that someone dumps a van-load of refuse in the park the very next day.

Write a news report about this, referring to the extract for information and ideas. Remember to give details that describe what happened, when, where, why and to whom.

MORETON Weekly

By

Unit 5 Resource 1

My dangerous creature poem

Use this grid to plan your own poem to describe the behaviour of a different dangerous animal.

The animal: _____

What does the animal look like?	
Where does it live? How does it sleep?	
What does the animal eat? How does it eat?	
How does the animal move? How would it react to seeing a human?	
How could you describe the animal in words that are usually used to describe people?	
How will you use rhyme?	

Unit 5 Resource 2

Shark facts

Research and make notes about the characteristics of sharks. You could then compare your notes with the information in the poem.

Types of shark

What sharks eat

What sharks look like

Where sharks live

How sharks behave

Unit 6 Resource 1

Getting the house to yourself

Plan your own short story or poem about someone who wants to get rid of someone else. What clever trick could they use to achieve this?

- Who will the characters be?
- What will the setting be?
- What will the plan or trick be?
- Will the plan be successful? What will happen in the end?

Unit 6 Resource 2

Spectre storyboard

Imagine you are directing a television adaptation of the poem. Plan how each shot will look. What camera positions will there be? What things will you show and when? What dialogue will you include?

1.	2.	3.

Dialogue:

4.	5.	6.

Dialogue:

7.	8.	9.

Dialogue:

Unit 7 Resource 1

Three diaries

Describe the events in the extract from each character's point of view. Write a short paragraph for each diary.

Mr B. Quiet's diary:

The complaining neighbour's diary:

Mr J. Trigger's diary:

Unit 7 Resource 2

A letter of complaint

Imagine that someone keeps dumping litter all over the school field. Write a formal letter of complaint to your local council requesting their support.

Ideas to think about:

- Introduce yourself and why you are writing.
- Use a polite, formal tone.
- Make it clear what you want the council to do.

The council's address:

Your address:

The date:

Dear Council Member,

Yours sincerely,

_____

Unit 8 Resource 1

What the Borrowers took

Choose six small items the Borrowers may have taken and illustrate ways these items may be used and what the Borrowers made from the items.

Item:	Item:
What the Borrowers made:	What the Borrowers made:
How they made it:	How they made it:

Item:	Item:
What the Borrowers made:	What the Borrowers made:
How they made it:	How they made it:

Item:	Item:
What the Borrowers made:	What the Borrowers made:
How they made it:	How they made it:

Unit 8 Resource 2

Kate's thoughts

Imagine you are Kate. Refer back to the extract and fill in the table below to show what you think at each point during the conversation with Mrs May.

"But I looked on the floor. Under the rug. Everywhere."
"Oh dear," exclaimed Mrs May lightly, "don't say they're in this house too!"
"Are there such things?"
"There can't be … And yet sometimes I think there must be."
"There was a reason for hatpins."
"But someone else saw one," cried Kate, "and you know about it. I can see you do!"

Unit 9 Resource 1

Finding the features

Label the start of the playscript with the features below.

| The character speaking | Stage directions | Character speech | The title of the play | Scene heading | Sound effects |

'The Lost Gardens' by Phil Osment

SCENE 1

(An Old Lady sits sleeping in a wheelchair.)

(Sound effect: birds singing)

MAYA   (offstage) Jack! Through here.

JACK   (offstage) Where are you?

MAYA   (offstage) Over here.

(Maya enters and sees the Old Lady.)

OLD LADY   (waking) Ahhhh! There you are at last.

MAYA   Pardon?

OLD LADY   I've been waiting for you.

Unit 9 Resource 2

Different characters

Complete these tables to help you to think about the four different characters in the scene. Look at how each of them acts, and decide what you think this means.

Character name:	
An example of something he/she said or did:	
What you think he/she is like:	

Character name:	
An example of something he/she said or did:	
What you think he/she is like:	

Character name:	
An example of something he/she said or did:	
What you think he/she is like:	

Character name:	
An example of something he/she said or did:	
What you think he/she is like:	

Unit 10 Resource 1

Smugglers

The poem is about smugglers. The poem is historical, but smugglers still exist today. Read the information below to understand more about this way of life.

Early smugglers

Smuggling is the name given to transporting something illegally from one place to another.

Smuggling has been going on for over 800 years, in England at least – ever since Edward I introduced taxes in 1275. Merchants were angry that the king wanted to take some of their money when they sold their goods, so they did it secretly.

At the time, the goods most frequently smuggled out of England for sale were wool, leather and grain. Wine was often smuggled into England from France.

As time went on, the most highly-taxed items continued to be smuggled into England. These were usually luxury goods from Europe. This would include the items mentioned in the poem: brandy, tobacco, lace – and expensive toys, too!

Some smugglers were ruthless and violent, and tried to make themselves a lot of money. Others were simply trying to provide for their families.

Modern-day smugglers

Smuggling still happens today.

Often, heavily-taxed goods are still a smuggler's cargo. However, a lot of the smuggling that causes the police the most trouble, and is seen on the news, is transporting illegal goods.

These illegal goods could include drugs and weapons. Sometimes even people are smuggled.

Some people want to be smuggled from one place to another because they can't move to a country legally. Other people are taken and smuggled against their will. They may be sold or used as very poorly-paid and poorly-treated workers.

Unit 10 Resource 2

Good or bad?

Reread the poem and sort its impressions of smugglers into the two columns. You could then add ideas from wider research to the table, too.

Reasons the smugglers were good	Reasons the smugglers were bad

Unit 11 Resource 1

Finding the beat

Look at the rhythm of the first verse. In the first two lines, the syllables that form the poem's beat are underlined.

Read the lines out loud and notice how they make the steady, rattling sound of a train chugging along.

Count the syllables in the other lines and underline the beats.

<u>Fas</u>ter than <u>fai</u>ries, <u>fas</u>ter than <u>witch</u>es,

<u>Bridg</u>es and <u>hou</u>ses, <u>hedg</u>es and <u>ditch</u>es;

And charging along like troops in a battle,

All through the meadows the horses and cattle;

All of the sights of the hill and the plain

Fly as thick as driving rain;

And ever again, in the wink of an eye,

Painted stations whistle by.

Robert Louis Stevenson

Unit 11 Resource 2

A mind map

Fill in the mind map to explore the feeling of being on a modern train.

Think carefully about what you may (or may not) see through the window. Might the sights seem to be moving, instead of the train?

Then compose your own poem, thinking carefully about the rhythm you will use.

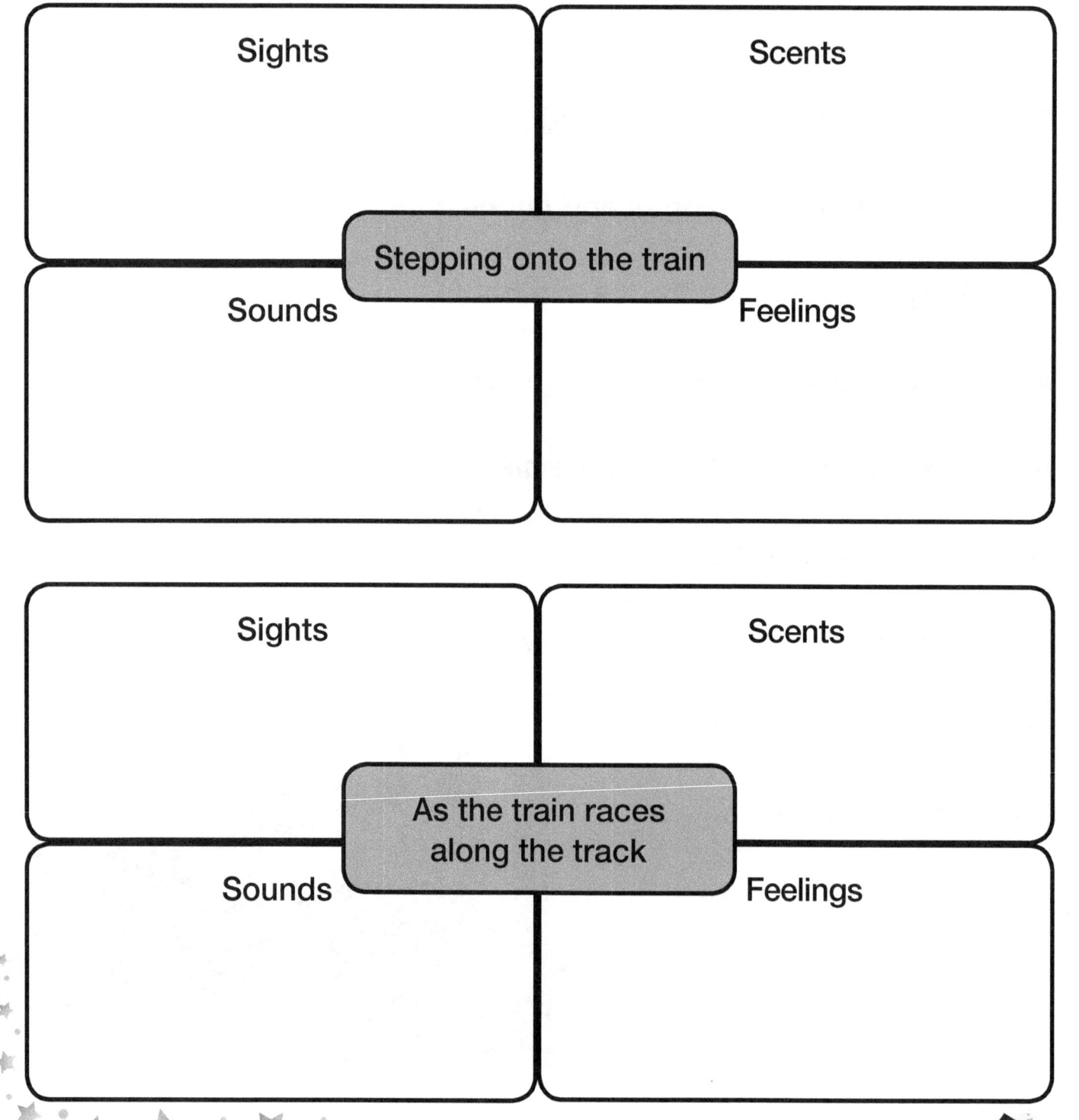

Sights	Scents

Stepping onto the train

Sounds	Feelings

Sights	Scents

As the train races along the track

Sounds	Feelings

Unit 12 Resource 1

Making a cup of tea

Read through these instructions, cut them out and put them in the correct order.

Then add:

- numbers to make the order clear
- diagrams to help the reader
- a title.

☐	Use the teaspoon to take the teabag out of the mug and put it in the bin.
☐	When the kettle has boiled, pour the hot water carefully into the mug.
☐	If you like, add milk, lemon and/or sugar to the tea.
☐	Boil the kettle.
☐	Make sure you have a kettle, some water, a mug, a teaspoon and a teabag (and milk, lemon and/or sugar, if you like).
☐	Put the teabag into the mug and put water into the kettle.
☐	Leave the teabag in the hot water for a few minutes (depending on how strong you would like the tea to be).

Unit 12 Resource 2

Writing a recipe

Use the template below to write your own set of instructions for a simple recipe (such as for making cheese on toast).

Title:	
Introduction paragraph:	

You will need:	Diagram:

1.

2.

3.

4.

5.

Unit 13 Resource 1

Quick quiz

Test your partner's knowledge about the Trojan War! Come up with five questions that the extract can answer. Then swap your quiz with a partner.

Questions:	Answers:
1.	
2.	
3.	
4.	
5.	

Unit 13 Resource 2

A Trojan comic strip

Retell some of the events in the extract as a comic strip. Look carefully at the number of panels in the template and where the thought and speech bubbles are placed.

Unit 14 Resource 1

Shen Nung's character

Use the text to create a profile of Shen Nung's character and achievements.

Picture	Name
	What he was the god of
	Physical description

What he invented

What he discovered

What he showed his people

What his wife discovered	What his wife became goddess of

How he died

Unit 14 Resource 2

An important discovery

Plan a piece of writing about someone else who discovered or developed something important. It could be an important scientist or a designer. The information could be entirely factual or, like the legend of Shen Nung, you could include some fictional parts.

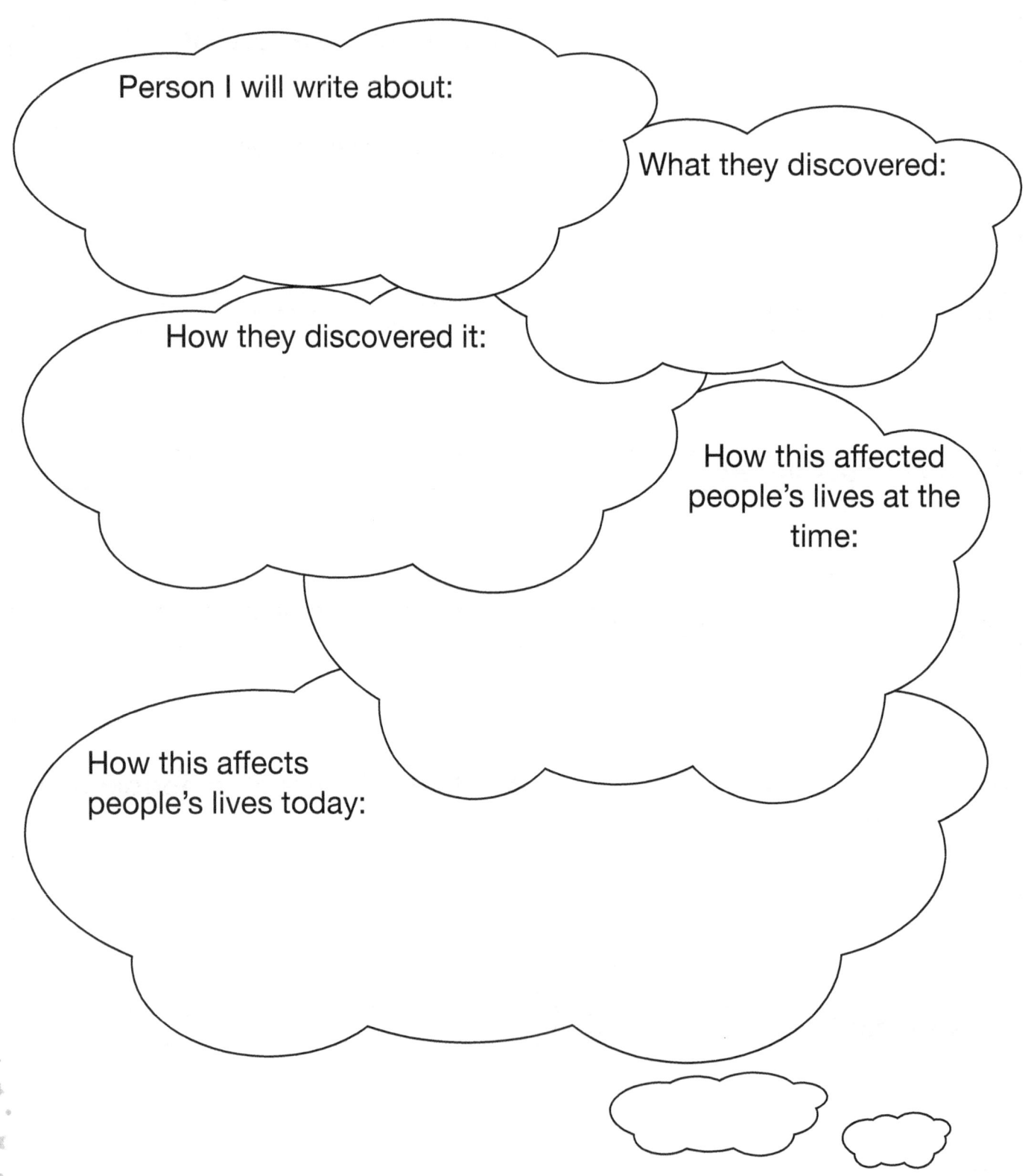

- Person I will write about:
- What they discovered:
- How they discovered it:
- How this affected people's lives at the time:
- How this affects people's lives today:

Unit 15 Resource 1

Questions about the USA

Read the passages below. Then create three questions about each passage. Ask a partner to answer them.

The presidency of the USA
Every four years, people in the USA who are aged over 18 can vote to elect their President and Vice President. The President of the USA is the head of the government of the United States, and is also commander-in-chief of the United States Armed Forces. He or she is considered to be one of the world's most powerful political figures. The President of the USA always lives in The White House, in Washington DC (the capital city of the USA).

Questions about this passage:

1.
2.
3.

The landscape of the USA
The USA is very large: it is the third biggest country in the world. Because of this, its landscape varies widely. In the USA, you could see: • snowy mountain ranges, in northern states like Montana • barren deserts, in central states like Nevada and Utah • tropical beaches, in southern states like Florida • dense forests, in states as different as snowy Alaska and sunny California. The USA also has famous natural landmarks, such as the Grand Canyon and the Mississippi River.

Questions about this passage:

1.
2.
3.

© HarperCollins*Publishers* Ltd 2017

Unit 15 Resource 2

Researching civil rights

Use this sheet to help you to research more about civil rights.

Plan four questions about civil rights you would like to answer.

1. _____

2. _____

3. _____

4. _____

Now do research to find the answers to your questions. Make notes here.

How will you present your information? Plan it here.

Unit 16 Resource 1

Mum and Gran

Imagine that Mum is trying to persuade Gran to give up her motorbike. Reread the extract carefully to gather information about each woman's character and what they may say then write a dialogue between them.

Unit 16 Resource 2

Gang rules

Imagine you are helping the leader of the 'Hedgehogs' to draw up some gang rules. Read the extract again carefully to make sure you use all of the information it gives about the gang, as well as using your imagination.

Gang name	Gang emblem

Gang motto	

Gang password	

In order to be in the gang, you must have:

In order to be in the gang, you must be:

Recommended clothing	Recommended hairstyles

Gang activities

Unit 17 Resource 1

The magical pearl

Answer the questions. Use details from the extract to help you.

- How do you think Xiao Sheng got the pearl?

- On whose land was the pearl found?

- What animal created the pearl?

- Who wanted the pearl from Xiao Sheng?

- Who does Xiao Sheng say the pearl's gifts belong to?

- How did Xiao Zheng use the pearl's magic?

- Where were Xiao Sheng and his mother hiding the pearl?

- How did Xiao Sheng try to protect the pearl?

- What happens if the pearl is swallowed?

Unit 17 Resource 2

The start of the story

Answer the questions in the planning grid to structure your thoughts about what must have happened in the story before the extract begins. Then write the start of the story.

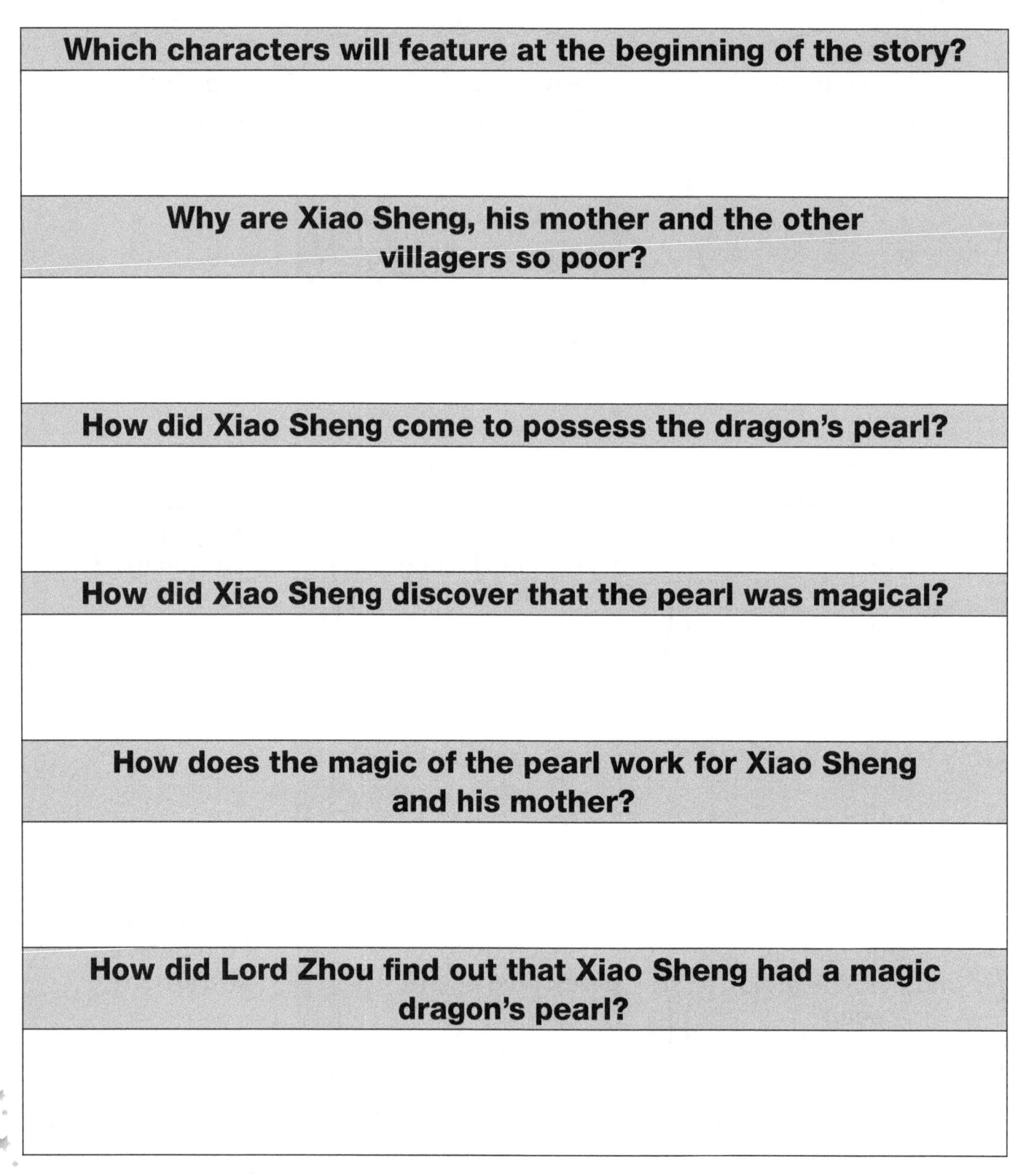

Which characters will feature at the beginning of the story?

Why are Xiao Sheng, his mother and the other villagers so poor?

How did Xiao Sheng come to possess the dragon's pearl?

How did Xiao Sheng discover that the pearl was magical?

How does the magic of the pearl work for Xiao Sheng and his mother?

How did Lord Zhou find out that Xiao Sheng had a magic dragon's pearl?

Unit 18 Resource 1

Comparing the poems

Use the table to help you compare the two poems.

What actions are being described?	
What on Earth?	**Progress Man!**

What are the problems caused?	
What on Earth?	**Progress Man!**

Who or what is to blame?	
What on Earth?	**Progress Man!**

How are the verses structured?	
What on Earth?	**Progress Man!**

Unit 18 Resource 2

My progress poem

Fill in the gaps to begin your own poem about progress, using 'Progress Man!' as a guide.

Firstly, think of the kind of progress you will describe. It doesn't have to be bad!

For example, you could write about people using computers rather than books.

Hurry now! *cried Progress*,

just see what I can do!

Watch my _____, feel my _____;

my _____ are great for you,

'cos I'm a swinging, singing,

racing, chasing, do-it-how-I-can,

I'm the swinging, singing,

racing, chasing Progress Man!

See me _____,

we need a _____!

You have some _____ already …?

Well, not enough, I say!

Unit 19 Resource 1

Quick quiz

Test your partner's knowledge about how to be an Ancient Greek! Come up with five questions that the extract can answer. Then swap your quiz with a partner.

Questions:	Answers:
1.	
2.	
3.	
4.	
5.	

Unit 19 Resource 2

Ancient instructions

The subheadings in the extract are instructions.

Choose one paragraph in the extract and break it down into five steps, presented as instructions.

For example, you could write instructions that:

- tell an Ancient Greek builder how to construct a polis

- tell the Mycenaeans what to do after the long period of bad weather

or

- suggest things Athenians could do for fun.

Step 1:	
Step 2:	
Step 3:	
Step 4:	
Step 5:	

Unit 20 Resource 1

Ade's reasons

Use the table below to explore the feelings and thoughts behind the facts of Ade's life. Find each fact in the extract, and read around it to find an emotion or opinion related to it.

Fact:	At first, I didn't want to join the Newham Rollers.
Emotion or opinion behind the fact:	
Fact:	I saw the wheelchairs that the GB basketball team used.
Emotion or opinion behind the fact:	
Fact:	I realised I wanted to be like the players on the team.
Emotion or opinion behind the fact:	
Fact:	I decided to try wheelchair basketball instead of football.
Emotion or opinion behind the fact:	
Fact:	I practised really hard.
Emotion or opinion behind the fact:	

Unit 20 Resource 2

Fact or opinion?

Read the extract again, and sort each piece of information given by Ade into one of these two columns.

Facts	Opinions and feelings